AMERICA'S HISTORIC

SHIPS

REPLICAS

& RESTORATIONS

AMERICA'S HISTORIC

SHIPS

REPLICAS

& RESTORATIONS

IRVIN HAAS

ARCO PUBLISHING COMPANY, INC.
219 Park Avenue South, New York, N.Y. 10003

PHOTO CREDITS

"Dick" Arikian; Sandra De Veau; Don Edwards; Russell A. Fawler; Melvin Fredeen; S. Durward Hoag; JZ Photo; Karl Kortum; Harper Leiper; Einars J. Mengis; Mystic Seaport; Naval Photographic Center; Lester D. Olin; Pennsylvania Historical and Museum Commission; Philadelphia Maritime Museum; Plimoth Plantation; San Francisco Maritime Museum; Shelburne Museum; Bill Schill; Smithsonian Institution; South Street Seaport Museum.

Published by Arco Publishing Company, Inc.
219 Park Avenue South, New York, N.Y. 10003

Library of Congress Catalog Card Number 74-30893
ISBN 0-668-3768-7

Printed in the United States of America

For the many pets we have had
who gave us love and pleasure
during their lifetimes.

FOREWORD

Our cavalier treatment of our past is not one of our most endearing qualities. We are too prodigal with our inheritance. Our life style almost forbids our looking back, and we literally bury our past at almost every chance. This casual treatment of time has caused countless historical and architectural treasures to disappear forever. All that we have to remind ourselves of our ancestors and how they lived their lives are some faded photographs or shredded old drawings. It is a sad heritage to leave to our progeny.

Only in recent years have a handful of people realized that if we did not attempt to preserve what we have left from periods remembered only in our history books, we would have nothing left at all. The preservation movement started unfortunately late. By the time professionals were trained, converts gathered, funds allocated, and organizations consolidated and functioning, far too many artifacts and sites were ground into the earth and covered over.

Now, the preservation movement is making up for much lost time. The expertise and dedication of its members are saving many old houses and making them available again for people to enjoy. Entire villages have been cataloged, restored, moved, reassembled, and, in some cases, reborn. Forts and battlefields crumbling from disuse have been cleared and restored and made part of our living history.

But there is one section of preservation that has been shockingly neglected. This is more tragic, considering that we have always been a voyaging and trading nation. Of the thousands of ships, both sail and steam, that have carried our flag into every port in the world, of all the vessels that brought settlers and wealth to our own shores, of the many ships that wrote so many thrilling chapters in our history and were in themselves things of grace and beauty, just a handful remain to be preserved and cherished. It is hard to believe that we are able at this date to save but a very few ships from destruction. They are all gone but for the few rotting in some out-of-the-way ports, eagerly searched for by a new breed of preservationist—one who goes down to the sea for ships.

It is doubtful that the ships described in this book would be anything other than scraps of wood or metal in waterfront junkyards if it were not for the heroic efforts of the National Maritime Historical Society and the almost superhuman efforts of such pioneers of maritime preservation as Peter Stanford, Karl Kortum, Carl Cutler, Robert Inverarity, and a few others. They have gone to incredible lengths to search out, recover, and renovate ships that they thought must be preserved. And none too soon, for it is estimated that there are only a dozen or so sailing vessels that can yet be saved for restoration—a pitiful legacy of the thousands that sailed the seas not too many years ago. There is still a little time to inventory the survivors, plan the feasibility of restoration, and somehow acquire the necessary funds to do the job. A task for giants! But these same maritime preservationists have achieved near-miracles before and are pre-pared to do so again. If they fail, the few vessels left will rot away. If they succeed, these vessels will remind us of the men who designed and built them and the many men who went to sea in them for the glory of us all.

My criteria for inclusion in this book are two-fold: the historical significance of the vessel, as gloriously exemplified by such ships as *Old Ironsides,* the *Constellation,* and the *Niagara*; and popularity with the viewing public. The vessels selected for the latter reason are not significant in an historical context, but nevertheless deserve, I feel, to be preserved as public museums. The various battlewagons of World War II are in that class, and even the replica of our English cousin, *H.M.S. Bounty,* is being visited by so many thousands in Florida that I couldn't commit the sin of omission in her case. The various Mississippi paddlewheelers have only local importance, but must also be included. At any rate, all of the ships described in the book are available for the great thrill of trodding their decks, peering into their quarters and holds, and recapturing the drama and glory of all these wonderful vessels—a feeling that I hope this book helps perpetuate.

Irvin Haas

CONTENTS

SHIPS

SHIPS

U.S.S. Arizona MEMORIAL, PEARL HARBOR.

U.S.S. ARIZONA MEMORIAL
Pearl Harbor, Hawaii

The U.S.S. Arizona Memorial spans the sunken hull of the battleship *U.S.S. Arizona* which rests in 38 feet of water at the bottom of Pearl Harbor. An enclosed bridge, touching no part of the ship itself, the 184-foot memorial is supported by two 250-ton concrete girders resting on 36 pre-stressed pilings. It varies from 28 feet at the center to 36 feet at the ends, and in height from 14 feet at the center to 21 feet at the ends.

The memorial is divided into three sections: the museum room, housing mementos from the ship; the assembly area, which can accommodate 200 persons for ceremonies; and the shrine room, where, on a large marble wall, are engraved the names of 1177 sailors and Marines who were killed on the *U.S.S. Arizona* in the Pearl Harbor attack.

The historic raid of December 7, 1941, in which the *Arizona* was sunk, was launched at 6 a.m. Honolulu time, from six Japanese aircraft carriers 200 miles northeast of Oahu. The first bombs fell at 7:55 a.m. and the attack ended about two hours later with the bulk of the United States naval might in the Pacific temporarily crippled. On that Sunday morning, 2341 American servicemen lost their lives and another 1143 were wounded. Of the 97 ships in Pearl Harbor that morning, 18 were sunk or damaged. The biggest prize of the day was the concentration of the seven battleships tied up along "Battleship Row": *U.S.S. California, U.S.S. Maryland, U.S.S. Oklahoma, U.S.S. Tennessee, U.S.S. West Virginia, U.S.S. Nevada,* and the *U.S.S. Arizona.*

The *Arizona* took five hits from large armor-piercing bombs. One of the bombs crashed through the deck near the Number 2 gun turret. A fire was started, apparently fed by oil from the forward tanks. The fire spread rapidly and soon reached the ship's powder magazines. The explosion which resulted caused the *Arizona* to erupt violently and sink to the bottom in less than nine minutes.

More than half of the 2113 Navy and Marine forces killed that day were aboard the *Arizona,* which had only 289 survivors out of the more than 1500 crew members. The ship lost 1104 sailors and 73 Marines, more than 1000 of whom remain trapped inside the sunken hull. Only 150 bodies were recovered.

Of the 18 ships sunk or damaged in Pearl Harbor, 15 were repaired and saw action during the war. The first major ship to return to action was the *U.S.S. Maryland,* less than three months after the attack. The three ships that did not see action were *Arizona, Oklahoma,* and *Utah.* Of the 33 ships comprising the Japanese task force, all but one were sunk during World War II.

The Navy operates two free boat tours of the site for the public—a visit to the *U.S.S. Arizona* Memorial and a one-hour tour of Pearl Harbor. The tours are offered on a first come, first served basis. The hours are from 9 a.m. to 3:30 p.m., Tuesday through Sunday, continuously except Sunday, when service is suspended for lunch from 12 to 1 p.m.

THE *Bounty* UNDER SAIL.

THE BOUNTY
St. Petersburg, Florida

Possibly one of the most publicized replicas ever built, the *Bounty* has attracted hundreds of thousands of visitors in her voyage around the world and in her permanent mooring in picturesque Vinoy Basin near St. Petersburg's Municipal Pier.

A faithful reproduction of the ship seized from Captain William Bligh in 1789 by mutiny leader Fletcher Christian, she was built by Metro-Goldwyn-Mayer for the filming of "Mutiny on the Bounty" in 1960. She was constructed in Lunenberg, Nova Scotia, her plans having been redrawn by MGM's marine architects from originals in England's National Maritime Museum. She was then sailed 7327 miles to the movie location in Tahiti.

The replica *Bounty* is a 480-ton vessel, having a 30-foot beam and a 14-foot draft with a length of 118 feet. More than 400,000 board feet of timber, most of it American oak from New Jersey, was used in her planking. Black spruce formed the bottom of her hull, and British Columbia fir her masts and yards. The biggest timber was used in the mainmast, which is 27 inches in diameter and 65 feet long. Height from the deck to the top of the mainmast is 103 feet.

Practically everyone in the town of Lunenberg, where shipbuilding crafts are still practiced, lent a hand in her building, including veteran shipwrights who could not resist coming out of retirement to work adze and trunnel on the frame of a wooden sailing ship. Their skills—many of

THE *Bounty* ON EXHIBIT IN ST. PETERSBURG.

them little used for generations—were sorely needed. So rare have they become that it is probable that the *Bounty* might be the last wooden ship of her kind to be built anywhere in the world.

She carries 18 sails, comprising 10,000 square feet of canvas, hand-stitched by local sailmakers. She had a crew of 25 when she made the Lunenberg-Tahiti trip, via the Panama Canal, in 33 sailing days. Her average speed was 9.3 knots and she covered more than 260 miles on her fastest day's run.

Her acting duties took up eight months at Tahiti, and then she sailed via Hawaii to Long Beach, California, in the fall of 1961. In the spring her crew rejoined her to fit her out for a tour of many of the world's best-known seaports. Late in September, 1962, she "returned" to England. She rode into Dover Harbor and was greeted with a 21-gun salute. Hours later she was escorted up the Thames and anchored with special Royal consent in the Pool of London. In a way, she had finally logged an end to the voyage left incomplete by an earlier, ill-fated *Bounty*.

In the summer of 1965, the newest stage in her career began. Amid a colorful South Seas setting, she became a permanent exhibit in Vinoy Basin, adjoining St. Petersburg's famous Million Dollar Pier. Visitors can now board the blue-hulled *Bounty*. From the carefully tarred rigging to the eighteenth-century furnishings below, the *Bounty* is every inch an ancient sailing vessel. Weatherworn sea charts, pewter tableware, wooden hogsheads, barrels, hammocks, and belongings of the seamen are in place. Christian's quarters are complete with a wax figure of the mutineer, and Bligh's large cabin is furnished with antiques from British vessels. On display, too, is a replica of the 23-foot longboat in which Christian set Bligh, with 18 loyal officers and men, adrift following the mutiny. With food, water, cutlasses, a sextant, and nautical tables that Christian provided, Bligh was able to sail the tiny craft 3618 miles to the Dutch East Indies. Here the survivors caught a ship for England. The original *Bounty* was sailed by Christian to the uncharted island of Pitcairn, where she was stripped and burned.

The *Bounty* is located at 345 Second Avenue, N.E. in St. Petersburg, Florida. It is open to visitors daily until 10 p.m. from Memorial Day to Labor Day and until 8 p.m. during the rest of the year.

U.S.S. COBIA
Manitowoc, Wisconsin

The *U.S.S. Cobia* was a member of the select company of World War II submarines which survived almost two years of action in the Pacific. Launched on November 28, 1943, at the Electric Boat Company shipyard in Groton, Connecticut, the *Cobia* was underway on her first war patrol on June 26, 1944. This was the first of her six war patrols during which she sank 13 Japanese ships. They ranged from a small junk to a 7800 ton cargo ship. All in all she accounted for a total of over 18,000 tons of Japanese shipping.

Cobia's most exciting battle took place February 26, 1945. In a running surface gun battle with two Japanese sea trucks, *Cobia* sent both to the bottom—but not before suffering her only fatality of the war. The *Cobia* also conducted intelligence surveys near enemy held islands and often rescued allied pilots and Japanese sailors.

In 1946, the *Cobia* was decommissioned and placed in the reserve fleet. She was put into commission again in 1951 to train submarine school students. She was brought to Milwaukee

THE *U.S.S. Cobia.*

in 1959 to serve as a training ship for the submarine reserve until July 1, 1970. She was donated to the Marine Museum at Manitowoc, Wisconsin, in 1969. On August 23, 1970, she was officially dedicated as a memorial to submariners throughout the world, and particularly to the men who were in the Silent Service of World War II.

You can enter the Control Room and hear the actual sounds of a submarine diving below the surface. You can hear the commands given, the gurgle of water, and the actual diving alarm as the submarine descends—all on tape. The Maneuvering Room contains the instruments that regulated the speed of the ship and the engines that shut down when the submarine dove. You can descend to the Torpedo Room and examine the sleeping quarters for 20 men and storage for

the cargo of torpedoes. In the engine room are the four main diesel engines which propel the ship. You can see the fresh water stills, the fuel oil purifiers, and the giant valves for taking in fresh air and removing the exhaust.

The length of the *Cobia* is 312 feet, her beam 27 feet, draft 15 feet, and displacement 1526 tons. She had a surface speed of 20.25 knots and a submerged speed of 8.75. She was designed for a depth of 300 feet. Her armament was ten torpedo tubes; one 3-inch/50-caliber; a single 20mm cannon; a single 40mm; two 50-caliber machine guns; two 30-caliber, and 24 torpedoes.

The flags flying from the deck of the *Cobia* are the flags of the participating countries in this International Memorial. A memorial book is mounted alongside each flag pole, with the names of the submariners recorded on it. The countries

CONTROL ROOM, *U.S.S. Cobia.*   MANEUVERING ROOM, *U.S.S. Cobia.*

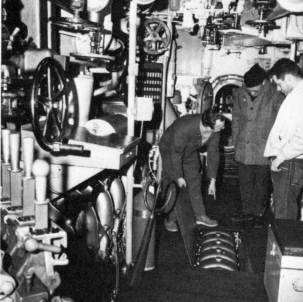

FORWARD TORPEDO ROOM, *U.S.S. Cobia.*   ENGINE ROOM, *U.S.S. Cobia.*

U.S.S. Cobia AT DOCK IN MANITOWOC, WISCONSIN "SUBMARINERS MEMORIAL."

represented are: the United States, Germany, Greece, Israel, Italy, Spain, Sweden, Turkey, and the United Kingdom.

The *U.S.S. Cobia* is docked at Manitowoc, Wisconsin, and is part of the Manitowoc Maritime Museum. Manitowoc is on Lake Michigan and can be reached by U.S. Highway 141. The Museum is open all year round, daily from 10 a.m. to 5 p.m. Adults pay $1.75 to board the *Cobia*, children 75 cents.

STERN VIEW OF THE *U.S.S. Constellation,* AT DOCK IN BALTIMORE.

U.S.S. CONSTELLATION
Baltimore, Maryland

In 1797, the year before Congress created the Navy Department, three frigates were launched: on July 10th, the 44-gun *United States* at Philadelphia; on September 7th, the 38-gun *Constellation* at Baltimore; and on September 20th, the 44-gun *Constitution* at Boston. Early in 1798, when war with France seemed inevitable, the three ships were not yet ready for sea duty, but in April of that year, under the command of Captain Thomas Truxton, the 1287-ton *Constellation* was put to sea, followed in July by the *United States* and the *Constitution*. X

Truxton had been designated to oversee construction of his ship when it was designated only as Frigate "E." He and the builder, David Stodder, supported by various government officials, made many modifications in the original plans in the interest of better design. Measuring 164 feet long and 40 feet wide, the ship could accommodate a complement of about 340 officers and men.

On the *Constellation's* "shakedown" cruise, during the undeclared war with France of 1798–1800, she convoyed a group of 60 merchantmen along the Atlantic coast. Sailing on to the West Indies, which was infested by French privateers that preyed on U.S. shipping, in 1799 she won her first victory by capturing the 44-gun French frigate *L'Insurgente,* the pride of the French Navy; and the following year she damaged the 56-gun *La Vengeance* so badly that she later sank. The *Constellation's* speed won her the nickname "The Yankee Racehorse." Captain Truxton pioneered in instituting for his seamen and marines a comprehensive shipboard training program, including gunnery practice, and establishing shipboard procedures.

After refitting at Norfolk, in 1800 the *Constellation* put out to sea under a new commander, Captain Alexander Murray. She served at Guadeloupe Station until 1801, by which time the United States had made peace with France. In 1802, she headed for Gibraltar and entered the renewed war against the Barbary pirates. From 1805 to 1812, while she was laid up "in ordinary" at the Washington Navy Yard, workmen rebuilt her and added a few inches to her beam. During the War of 1812, though the British blockade confined her to the Chesapeake Bay, she had a part in thwarting a British invasion attempt at Craney Island, Hampton Roads. In 1815, helping in the final subjugation of the Barbary pirates in the Mediterranean, during her last ship-to-ship battle, she led a group of four ships that captured the 46-gun frigate *Mashuda*.

Between 1815 and 1841, the *Constellation* served at various foreign stations, but in 1828 was laid up in Norfolk where, in 1831, she was again repaired and rebuilt, her stern being rounded. During the period 1841–1844 the *Constellation* cruised around South America to the Orient as the flagship of Commodore Lawrence Kearny, in command of the East Indian Squadron, whose mission was the protection of U.S. interests in China against British encroachment. In the course of negotiations with Chinese officials, Kearny obtained for the United States commercial privileges similar to those the officials had granted to England. The negotiations paved the way for the Open Door Policy in China. En route home, Kearny stopped at the Sandwich (Hawaiian) Islands to protest English attempts to take them over. He entertained King Kamehameha aboard the *Constellation* and promised U.S. support for Hawaiian independence. Britain finally refused the cession and Kearny returned home.

From 1845 to 1853 the *Constellation*, out-

X SEE PAGE 82!

BOW OF THE *U.S.S. Constellation.*

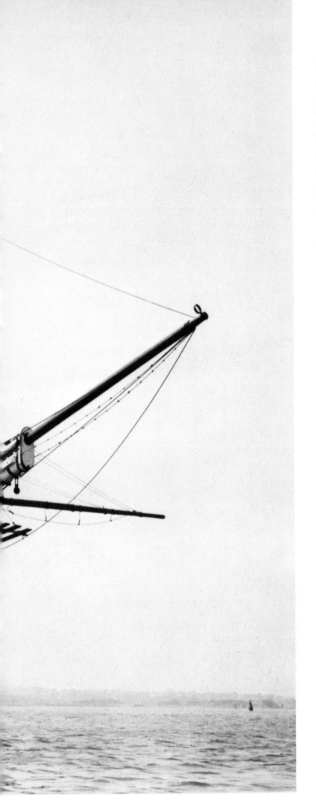

moded as a fighting ship, was laid up "in ordinary" at Norfolk. During the next two years, workmen at Norfolk's Gosport Navy Yard lengthened her by 12 feet and rebuilt her as a sloop-of-war, or corvette. After cruising for a few years in Mediterranean and Cuban waters, she was decommissioned at Boston in 1858. The following year, recommissioned, she sailed to Africa to serve in the slave trade blockade. In 1861, unaware that the Civil War had broken out, she made the first capture of a Confederate vessel on the high seas—the slaver *Triton* out of Charleston. She remained in European waters until 1864, when the Navy returned her to the United States for blockade duty.

During her final and uneventful years, the *Constellation* carried relief supplies to Ireland during the famine of 1880; served as a training and gunnery ship during World War I; and saw duty as a relief flagship of the Atlantic Fleet during World War II—at the behest of President Roosevelt, an avid student of the ship's history. After the war a citizen's group saved her from scrapping and Congress authorized her return to Baltimore, her place of origin.

As much as a ship of her age can be, the *Constellation* is a splendid example of a warship that was launched back in 1797. Perhaps 35 percent of the total hull is original, consisting of live-oak timber and pig-iron ballast. The alterations were the normal reworking of the basic structure to maintain the effectiveness of the ship throughout the years and do not impair her historical integrity.

She is located at Pier 4, Pratt Street, Baltimore, Maryland. She is open to the public from Labor Day to June 19, Monday to Saturday, 10 a.m. to 4 p.m.; Sunday from 12 noon to 5 p.m. From June 20th to Labor Day, Monday to Saturday from 10 a.m. to 6 p.m.; Sunday from 12 noon to 6 p.m. Adults pay $1.00 to board her, children 50 cents.

U.S.S. CONSTITUTION
Boston, Massachusetts

"Old Ironsides" is a stirring symbol of the early years of the U.S. Navy and the great age of fighting sail. The *Constitution* was the last of three frigates whose construction began in 1794. She was launched at Boston, on ~~September 20,~~ *OCT. 21,* 1797, and was the last of the three to be put to sea. Launched before her were the *United States* and the *Constellation*. "Old Ironsides" served with distinction through the War of 1812. She has never been decommissioned. *WRONG (1883–1931)*

Constructed in Boston between 1794 and 1797, she was 175 feet long had a 43½-foot beam, and a displacement of 1576 tons. She mounted 44 guns. Her timbers were of live oak, red cedar, and hard pine. Paul Revere and Son sheeted the lower hull with copper. During the years 1801–05, as the flagship of Commodore Edward Preble, she served in the War with the Barbary States. She attacked Tripoli five times, and the peace treaty ending the war was signed on her deck.

It was in the War of 1812 that the *Constitution* won undying fame. A few weeks after the war broke out in June, while en route to New York, she narrowly escaped a British squadron in a demonstration of brilliant seamanship by her commander, Captain Isaac Hull. Later that summer, while returning from a successful raiding cruise into Canadian waters, she defeated the British frigate *Guerriere* in a hard-fought, close-range duel. The victory thrilled the nation. According to tradition, during the engagement a seaman, on seeing the enemy's shots rebounding from her sides, dubbed the ship "Old Ironsides."

In December, 1812, under the command of Commodore William Bainbridge, the *Constitution* met the British frigate *Java* off the coast of Brazil. The two ships momentarily jammed to-

U.S.S. Constitution IN BOSTON HARBOR.

gether and the crew of the *Constitution* beat off a British boarding party. As the ships parted, the *Java's* mainmast crashed down and she was forced to surrender. For long periods during the remainder of the war, the increasingly vigilant British blockade kept the *Constitution* confined along the Atlantic coast, but in December, 1814, she escaped to sea. In February of the following year, two months after the Treaty of Ghent had been negotiated, she met two British warships off Spain—the *Cyane* and the *Levant,* whose combined gunpowder was superior. The *Constitution,* however, used her concentrated firepower to advantage and in a few hours captured them. This was her last battle, a fitting end to a career of glory that was to earn her a noble place in our nation's history.

In 1828, when the ship was condemned as unseaworthy and on the brink of destruction, she was saved in part by Oliver Wendell Holmes's poem, "Old Ironsides," which aroused public sentiment. Used as a training ship thereafter, she was rebuilt or partially rebuilt in 1833, 1871–77, and 1906.

She floats today in the harbor in which she was originally launched and has undergone such extensive restoration that she may be said to be a reconstruction. *NOT TRUE* During the course of several rebuildings, her original rotting timbers were removed. During the period 1927–1930, final restoration took place. Bearing her original lines and characteristics, she is a thrilling picture of a fighting frigate.

Her crew today, all non-rated men picked for this duty out of boot camp for a one-year tour, are responsible for keeping the ship presentable at all times. Each year she is turned around to keep the sun from warping the masts and spars. This is the occasion for a gala ceremony attended by high-ranking Navy officers and state and federal dignitaries. "Old Ironsides" is also the flagship for the Commandant, First Naval District, and is constantly involved with honors and ceremonies.

The *Constitution* is berthed in the Boston Naval Shipyard. She is open daily from 9:30 a.m. to 4 p.m. There is no admission charge.

FALLS OF CLYDE
Honolulu, Hawaii

In her 90-year life span, the *Falls of Clyde* has followed three distinct sea careers. Built principally for world tramping, an industry then (1878) dominated by Clyde shipowners, she was designed to carry a larger cargo and sail with a smaller crew than was the norm. She was the first of nine vessels, all named for waterfalls in Scotland, comprising the famous Falls Line. The *Falls of Clyde,* from 1879 to 1899, made 70 voyages to ports around the world carrying general and bulk cargo such as lumber, jute, cement, and wheat.

The ship's second career began in December,

1898, at San Francisco, when Honolulu Marshal A. M. Brown bought her for $25,000. Brown was in reality acting as an agent for William Matson, who through Brown could attempt to secure Hawaiian registry for the *Falls of Clyde.* With the expected annexation of the Hawaiian Islands, the ship would then come under American registry. Under a temporary Hawaiian registry issued in San Francisco, she arrived in Honolulu on January 20, 1899, the first four-masted iron ship with yards on each mast that ever came into the harbor flying the Hawaiian flag.

About $15,000 was spent to change the *Falls*

Falls of Clyde.

of Clyde from ship to bark rig, add a deck house and chart house, and rearrange the after quarters for passengers. The vessel, then the largest in the sugar trade, was placed in regular passenger and cargo service between Hilo and San Francisco. From 1899 to 1907, over 60 voyages were made between these ports. Sailing time averaged 17 days, each way.

William Matson soon formed the Matson Navigation Company, whose seven-star flag represented the original vessels of the line, including the *Falls of Clyde*. He began introducing steamers into his fleet and, in a less known activity, became a pioneer in the transportation of oil.

The *Falls of Clyde* became a maritime rarity when she was converted to a sailing oil tanker in 1907 to begin her third career. Built into the ship were ten large tanks, the expansion trunks of which were along the port and starboard sides of the deck. Heavy-duty pumps and a second steam boiler to operate them were installed. Sold to the Associated Oil Company, she continued to serve the Islands, sailing mainly between Gaviota, California, and Honolulu, with 756,000 gallons of oil. Discharging was usually done at the Oahu Railway and Land Company's Pier 16. Small quantities of miscellaneous dry cargo were carried and bulk molasses was often loaded at Honolulu.

During 1921–22, the *Falls of Clyde* made two charter trips carrying oil from Texas to Denmark, one voyage to Buenos Aires, and another to Panama. She then went to San Pedro, California, where she was rigged down to a barge, but with her lower masts intact. Towed to Ketchikan, Alaska, she was operated by the General Petroleum Company as a floating fuel depot until 1958.

A private owner bought the ship and took her to Seattle. From 1959 to 1962, several cities, including Seattle, San Pedro, Long Beach, Philadelphia, and even Honolulu, tried to buy the vessel for museum purposes. Finally, in 1963, the people of Hawaii, by public subscription, raised over $25,000 in four weeks and bought the *Falls of Clyde* just weeks before she was to be sunk as a log breakwater at Vancouver, British Columbia. The U.S. Navy's fleet tug *Moctobi* towed the *Falls of Clyde* from Seattle on her last trip home to Honolulu.

Ownership and management was assumed by the B.P. Bishop Museum in the summer of 1968. Her restoration includes aspects of each of her careers. Her general outboard restoration is that of the original appearance and decoration as a four-masted full-rigged ship, the world's only such survivor. The inboard features of the ship display the sole surviving example of a sailing oil tanker. The various earlier changes made by Matson are preserved as well. *Falls of Clyde* is considered to have one of the finest and best preserved hulls of all museum ships. Her documented background and authentic restoration make her an historic site worth visiting.

Falls of Clyde is located on Pier 5, Honolulu Harbor, Ala Moana Boulevard in downtown Honolulu. Admission hours are from 10 a.m. to 11 p.m. daily. She is closed on Thanksgiving and Christmas Day. Adults pay $1.50 to board her; children from 6 to 17 pay 50 cents.

CREW'S QUARTERS, *Falls of Clyde*.

OFFICER'S/PASSENGERS' SALOON, *Falls of Clyde*.

GAZELA PRIMEIRO
The Philadelphia Maritime Museum
Philadelphia, Pennsylvania

The *Gazela Primeiro* is the last of the Portuguese square-rigged fishing fleet. Built in 1883 at Cacilhas, Portugal, she sailed from Portugal to the fabulous cod fishing area off Newfoundland called the Grand Banks. She was acquired by the Philadelphia Maritime Museum in 1970 and was sailed by a volunteer crew from Lisbon to Philadelphia in 1971.

Each spring, for over a century, after the "Blessing of the Fleet" at the Church of Jeronimos in Lisbon, the fleet would sail for the Grand Banks. On the fishing grounds every fisherman would rise about four in the morning and scramble into his small boat, called a dory, leave the mothership, and sail or row away. A dory held one fisherman and he would play out his half-mile long fishing line, remove the thirty- to sixty-pound codfish, rebait and reset the line again, often catching 1000 pounds of fish a day. The fisherman would return to the ship only to unload his catch or when the sun began to slip below the horizon. At times when weather or fog was bad the captain of the ship would recall the dories by hoisting a flag or blasting a signal on the ship's horn. It was at least a twelve-hour fishing day but after returning to the mothership, the fisherman still had to clean fish as long as there were fish to be cleaned and help put them down in salt in the hold. The doryman fished for five or six months, day in, day out, in fog and rain, until the ship's hold was filled. Such was the daily life aboard the *Gazela Primeiro*.

This three-masted barkentine has sailed for nearly one hundred years to the North Atlantic codfish grounds. She is a barkentine because she has three masts with square sails on the foremast and fore and aft sail on the main and mizzen mast. Her overall length is 177 feet 10 inches, her beam is 27 feet, her draught loaded is 17 feet 6 inches, her foremost height from the deck is 93 feet 4 inches, her gross tonnage is 324 and her net tonnage is 221. Her frames are made of stone pine. Her hull planking and floors are of maritime pine and her hull is also copper sheathed. Her main engine is a 4-cylinder Mannheim Diesel delivering 180 BHP. Her speed under power is 6 knots. She has 13 sails and a sail area of 990 square yards. Her crew numbered from 30 to 37 men and she carried more than 31 dories.

On deck, the 14-foot, one-man dories were carried in stacks of four or six. Forward is the old hand windlass used to hoist the anchor; it is now supplemented by a small diesel engine. In the forward deckhouse the cook provided a constant flow of cod prepared in a great variety of ways. The small hatch aft of the cookhouse is to the refrigerated bait locker. Next are two entrances to the hold, which had a capacity of over 700,000 pounds. Further aft is the companionway to the tiny salon and four cabins for the ship's officers. At the stern is the pilot house where the course of the ship is directed.

Below decks and at the bow is the forecastle, called "the rancho" by the Portuguese, which is the crew's quarters containing a small cabin for the cook and 21 bunks and a table. At midship is the main hold where the fish were packed in

THE BARKENTINE *Gazela Primeiro* IS THE LAST OF THE PORTUGUESE SQUARE-RIGGED FISHING FLEET.

Gazela Primeiro.

salt for the homeward voyage, then the engine room, followed by four small cabins in the stern for the officers.

The *Gazela Primeiro* is located at the foot of Vine Street on the Delaware River in Philadel- phia. In the summer she can be visited every day of the week from noon to 5 p.m. In the winter she is open weekends only from noon to 5 p.m. Adults pay $1.00 to board, children 50 cents.

MEMORIAL ROOM EXHIBITS, *U.S.S. Massachusetts.*

U.S.S. MASSACHUSETTS
Battleship Cove,
Fall River, Massachusetts

Two months after the keel of the "Big Mamie" was laid down in Quincy, Massachusetts, on July 20, 1939, Germany invaded Poland. Days later, Great Britain and France declared war on Germany. In the Far East, Japan had landed in Shanghai in 1937 and was eyeing further Pacific conquests. The *Massachusetts* was being rushed to completion when the Japanese attack on Pearl Harbor plunged America into the war. The 35,000-ton ship officially joined the U.S. Navy on May 12, 1942, at the start of a 39-month fighting career during which she would earn the reputation as "Workhorse of the Fleet."

Her first wartime action was at Casablanca, supporting Operation Torch, the first major American amphibious assault against the European-Axis powers: the invasion of North Africa. Torch was the largest overseas expedition that had ever been attempted in the history of man. In November of 1942, "Big Mamie" was designated flagship for Admiral H. Kent Hewitt's Western Naval Task Force which was to land some 35,000 Army troops near Casablanca. She rendezvoused with the Task Force on November 28th. The armada stretched over 800 miles of submarine-infested waters. In Casablanca Harbor, the newest battleship in the French Navy, *Jean Bart,* about the same tonnage as the *Massachusetts* and with four 15-inch guns in the forward turret, aided by modern range-finding equipment, was a formidable enemy. "Big Mamie" fired nine 16-inch salvos and hit the French ship five times in rapid succession. A sixth hit jammed *Jean Bart's* forward gun turret and silenced the entire main battery. At 10:35 a.m. the *Massachusetts* engaged a French destroyer of the *L'Alcyon* class. Four hits were landed on the destroyer's stern and she rolled over and sank.

U.S.S. Massachusetts AT BERTH.

The *Massachusetts* received a shell from one of the shore batteries on the main deck that exploded between decks, and two more hits landed on her starboard quarter near one of the 20mm gun mounts. There were no casualties and the fires were extinguished. A cease-fire was reached with the French in North Africa on November 11th. Operation Torch was an unqualified success.

The *Massachusetts* spent the end of 1942 in the Boston Naval Shipyard and on February 6, 1943, she sailed to join the War in the Pacific. She joined the battleship forces commanded by Rear Admiral Willis A. Lee and operated with the American carrier *Saratoga* and the British carrier *Victorious*, offering protection against air and surface raiders as they jointly guarded the Navy's convoy lanes in the South Pacific. In November she protected the carrier group whose planes were striking at Makin, Tarawa, and Apanama in the Gilbert Island group. She had her first brush with Japanese planes on Thanks-

giving evening, destroying two of them. Through the night and the next day the Task Force fought back repeated attacks by Japanese torpedo planes. They returned just after dark the next day and one of the largest night air attacks the Pacific Fleet had ever experienced was successfully beaten back after hours of fighting. The Task Force steamed north and launched air strikes against Kwajalein.

Two years and one day after the attack on Pearl Harbor, the *Massachusetts* struck her first blow at Japanese-occupied territory. On December 8, 1943, she fired 136 16-inch shells and 400 five-inch projectiles into the island of Nauru from a position of less than a mile offshore. On February 17, 1944, the Force attacked the "impregnable" Japanese stronghold at Truk. The enemy naval losses alone were two light cruisers, four destroyers, two sub chasers, two tenders, an aircraft ferry, 24 auxiliaries, and six tankers. More than 250 enemy aircraft were damaged or destroyed. Truk was no longer useful and the

MEMORIAL ROOM OF THE *U.S.S. Massachusetts.*

enemy was badly shaken and hurt.

The Fleet steamed westward to launch air attacks against the Marianas. On February 21st and 22nd, the *Massachusetts* was hit with the longest sustained air attack she had encountered to date. Her men spent two days and nights at battle stations. Late in March she took part in a raid deep within the Japanese held islands as the Fleet struck Palau, Yap, Ulithi, and Woleai in

the Carolines. The next month "Big Mamie" headed south to take part in the April invasion of Hollandia—an operation which isolated 60,000 Japanese troops on New Guinea. Before leaving for the States, she took part in the air and surface bombardment at Ponape.

She had been in the Pacific for 15 months and celebrated her second birthday in Pearl Harbor. She got a much-needed overhaul and in two

CHILDREN ABOARD THE *U.S.S. Massachusetts.*

months sailed for the Hawaiian Operating Area. On October 10th she was off Okinawa, supporting the Fleet Operations against the big island base only 300 miles from the Japanese home islands. From October 22nd through October 27th, she took part in one of the greatest sea battles the world had ever seen—the decisive Battle of Leyte Gulf. The entire Japanese Fleet was committed to one last desperate gamble to wipe out the transports around Leyte. They planned a three-pronged attack on the U.S. Fleet, but from the beginning the battle went against them. The carrier aircraft in the *Massachusetts* force sank four Japanese aircraft carriers, a cruiser, and a destroyer. The Japanese failure spelled the doom of Japanese sea power.

On December 17th, the worst typhoon the Navy had seen during the war damaged the *Massachusetts* and sank three destroyers. In company with other fast battleships, she bombarded Okinawa on March 24th, the "Last Stepping Stone" to Japan herself. On July 1, 1945, "Big Mamie" sailed for what was to be the final offensive of the War—the Third Fleet's Operation against Japan. On July 14th she joined the bombardment unit that included the battleships *South Dakota* and *Indiana* and the heavy cruisers *Quincy* and *Chicago,* accompanied by nine destroyers. In coordination with air strikes, the naval gun fire force bombarded the home island of Japan for the first time. The target was the second largest iron and steel producing center in Japan, the Imperial Ironworks at Kamaishi. Shells struck the blast furnaces, open-hearth works, factory buildings, and fuel storage tanks. There was no opposition and the target was destroyed. On August 9th, when a second atomic bomb destroyed Nagasaki, the *Massachusetts* returned to Kamaishi and fired what was probably the last 16-inch shell fired in anger in World War II. The end of the War found the *Massachusetts* cruising in the waters off Japan.

After picking up passengers from different ships in the waters south of Tokyo, she steamed for the United States and arrived in the Puget Sound Naval Shipyard on September 13, 1945, after a 5000 mile, nonstop voyage. She became inactive on May 20, 1946, at the Norfolk Naval Shipyard. She was decommissioned on March 27, 1947, and assigned to the Norfolk Group, U.S. Atlantic Reserve Fleet.

Three years of fund raising and effort by schoolchildren, former crew members, and Massachusetts citizens paid off when the proud veteran was transferred from the Navy to the *U.S.S. Massachusetts* Memorial Committee. Her final berth at Battleship Cove makes her available for all to visit this historic battleship now flying the Fighting Flag of the Massachusetts Navy. Moored next to her and on view is the World War II submarine, *U.S.S. Lionfish.*

The *Massachusetts* is 680 feet 10 inches long. Her extreme beam is 108 feet 2 inches, and has a mean draft of 29 feet 3 inches. She is 35,000 tons and had a designed speed of 27 knots. Her original armament is 9 16-inch 45-caliber guns; 20 5-inch 38-caliber guns; 15 quadruple 40mm anti-aircraft gun mounts, and 35 20mm anti-aircraft guns. She has two Kingfisher spotting planes on aft catapults and the maximum thickness of her armor is 18 inches. Her total horsepower was 130,000 powered by high pressure (600 pounds per square inch), superheated (850° F) steam turbines. She has four propellers and two rudders.

The battleship *Massachusetts* and submarine *Lionfish* are berthed at the State Pier in Fall River, Massachusetts, at the interchange of Interstate Routes 195 and 138. One admission ($2 for adults, $1 for children) entitles a visit to both the battleship and the submarine. They are open year round from May through October from 9 a.m. to 5 p.m.; from November through April from 9 a.m. to 4:30 p.m. They are closed Thanksgiving and Christmas Day.

Mayflower II, BERTHED AT STATE PIER, PLYMOUTH.

MAYFLOWER II
Plymouth, Massachusetts

The *Mayflower II* is a full-scale replica of the type of ship which brought the settlers from England to America in 1620. In the following years other vessels, most of them smaller than the *Mayflower,* brought additional settlers and supplies to this English outpost and carried back products of the New World which were intended to pay the costs of the Pilgrim venture. The Pilgrims used a shallop on trading and fishing trips to gather exports. There is a full-scale model of such a vessel alongside the *Mayflower II.* The sea was the fastest and safest highway they had.

There is little technical information known about the original *Mayflower.* The designer of this replica incorporated the few references in Governor Bradford's account of the voyage to Plymouth into information from his research on merchant vessels of the period to guide the recreation of an early seventeenth-century vessel.

Exhibits aboard the *Mayflower II* show what life was like on the 1620 voyage of 66 days, when the vessel was crowded with 102 passengers, about 25 crewmen, and enough supplies necessary for the long voyage to plant a colony 3000 miles from home. What an incredible cargo for a vessel measuring only 104 feet long, 78 feet 8 inches at the waterline, a beam of 25½ feet and a draft of 13 feet!

On board, wax figures portray the daily tasks of life aboard a ship in the seventeenth century. The Captain is charting a course, a seaman is working the windlass. The cook is cooking for the crew and, in the Tiller flat, an entire family, including baby, shows the crowded condition below decks. The signing of the Mayflower Compact on November 1, 1620, is commemorated in the Great Cabin of *Mayflower II.*

How was it possible for this small vessel to sail directly across the Atlantic at the worst time of the year, alone and without a convoy, and, by

Mayflower II AND SHALLOP.

Mayflower II UNDER SAIL.

the standards of the day, make excellent time—
66 days? What kind of navigational equipment
would the Captain of the *Mayflower* have had
and just how accurate would it be?

Here is a compendium by Commander David
W. Waters, English navigational authority, of a
navigator's equipment in the early 1600's:

"Compass, rough weight and line for soundings,

cross staff (or astrolabe) for measuring celestial
angles, a fairly good table of the sun's distances
north or south of the equator by seasons and
times, a table of corrections for the altitude of
Polaris and floats to be thrown ahead and timed
in passage alongside to estimate speed of the
ship. When you consider these simple navigational
instruments available to Captain Jones of the

Mayflower, he did exceptionally well in making his landfall off Cape Cod—not too far off his plotted course for the mouth of Hudson's River."

The 181-ton replica of the original *Mayflower* was built in England and sailed across the Atlantic in 1957 with a crew of 33 men under the command of Captain Alan Villiers. Their crossing took 53 days.

The *Mayflower II* is berthed at State Pier on Water Street in Plymouth, Massachusetts. Visitors can also see Plymouth Rock, a short distance from the vessel, and visit Pilgrim Village, only two and one-half miles away on scenic Route 3A. The ship can be visited from April to November, daily and holidays, from 10 a.m. to 5 p.m.; during the summer months from 10 a.m. to 6 p.m. Adults board her for $1.00, children 50 cents.

CUTAWAY VIEW—ORIGINAL *Mayflower.*

FLAGSHIP NIAGARA
Erie, Pennsylvania

On September 10, 1813, an American squadron of nine small ships, six of them constructed at Erie—which was far from the source of supply—challenged the British fleet on Lake Erie. In the bloody duel that followed, the upstart American Navy, which had already covered itself with glory on the high seas, removed the British threat to the Northeast, opened the supply lines to the military in Ohio, and raised hopes throughout an apprehensive and divided nation.

One hundred years after the battle, in 1913, the remains of the historic brig *Niagara* were raised from Lake Erie and the ship rebuilt. Although twice repaired since, the brig retains a

RECONSTRUCTION OF THE *U.S.S. Niagara,* COMMANDER PERRY'S SECOND FLAGSHIP DURING THE WAR OF 1812, IS A SQUARE-RIGGED 34-GUN WARSHIP.

long section of its original keel. With its full rigging and its cannon, the ship looks today much as the historians believe it did in the protected harbor at Erie, waiting to sail into battle.

The construction of this small fleet was a remarkable feat in itself. Erie was a small and isolated community separated by long distances and uncertain transportation from the centers of manufacture. Skilled craftsmen had to be imported and were difficult to recruit. Carpenters, blockmakers, blacksmiths, shipjoiners, caulkers, boat builders, and laborers were brought in, a few from Pittsburgh, many from Philadelphia.

Materials and manufactured goods were difficult to obtain. Erie had no iron. Some was obtained from Meadville and Pittsburgh. Other towns were ransacked for every available piece. Rigging and anchors were manufactured in Pittsburgh, the sails in Philadelphia. Cannon were obtained from Washington, D.C., and much of the shot from Pittsburgh. As there were no sawmills, the task of cutting, hewing, and squaring the timber was done by hand.

Daniel Dobbins, a native of Lewistown, Pennsylvania, and a veteran shipmaster on the Great Lakes, was assigned the task of building a fleet on Lake Erie by the Navy Department in Washington. He was not a shipbuilder, yet he masterfully organized and directed the building until experienced designers and supervisors could arrive. He worked tirelessly and traveled far to obtain men and materials.

In March of 1813, Commander Oliver Hazard Perry arrived from his home in Rhode Island and assumed command. His problems were not limited to construction. The government failed to supply enough men to man the ships, and many of those who were sent were diverted by Perry's superior to duty elsewhere. In the end, Perry was forced to assign militiamen to reinforce the ships' crews.

On August 1st, Perry and his men began the difficult job of floating the six small boats over the sand bar at the entrance of the bay. The

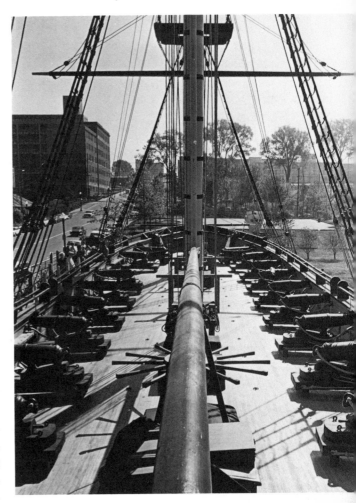

FLAGSHIP *Niagara.*

Niagara and the *Lawrence,* the two largest brigs, were floated across the bar with difficulty, on empty tanks, or "camels."

Captain Barclay's British fleet and Commander Perry's had about equal firepower. The *Lawrence,* with Perry aboard, challenged the largest of the British ships, while the *Niagara,* under the command of Commander Jesse D. Elliott, for reasons still uncertain, did not advance. Nevertheless, the men of the *Lawrence* held fast and delivered a furious bombardment on the enemy. With four out of five dead or

wounded, Perry, his thirteen-year-old brother, and four sailors escaped by boat to the *Niagara*, which was still fresh, brought it into the line of battle, and defeated the enemy.

In the calm that followed, Commander Perry wrote his report to Secretary of Navy Paul Hamilton, "We have met the enemy and they are ours: Two ships, two Brigs, one Schooner and one Sloop."

The *Niagara* was put to other uses for a few years, but decay set in and after a while it was allowed to sink into Misery Bay at Erie. In 1913, to celebrate the centennial of the battle, it was decided to bring the old ship up from its grave. The timbers of the keel were found to be well preserved and were incorporated into the reconstruction. Unfortunately, a detailed plan of the ship had not been preserved. The *Niagara* is a square-rigged warship with two masts, the foremast standing 92 feet in height and the mainmast 100 feet. On its fighting deck the brig carries 18 cannonades and 32-pound guns for close-in fighting. These cannonades were cast in Erie in 1913 for the reconstruction. The two long guns on the bow are called chasers and are 12-pounders. These guns date from the time of the battle, but it is uncertain whether they were carried on the *Niagara*.

On the quarter deck below are the quarters for the captain, the cramped cabins of the ship's officers and midshipmen, the dispensary, the boatswain's storeroom, the gunner's storeroom, the sail bin, the fireplace and hearth, and other facilities. The sailors and men were quartered on this deck, where they slept in hammocks.

The *Niagara* is at the foot of State Street in Erie, Pennsylvania. State Road 8 and U.S. Highways 19, 20, and 90 lead to the site. The facility is open in summer from 8:30 a.m. to 5 p.m. weekdays except Monday; 1 p.m. to 5 p.m. on Sunday. In winter it is open from 9 a.m. to 4:30 p.m. on weekdays except Monday; Sunday from 1 p.m. to 4:30 p.m. There is no admission charge.

FLAGSHIP *Niagara*.

U.S.S. North Carolina.

U.S.S. NORTH CAROLINA BATTLESHIP MEMORIAL
Wilmington, North Carolina

At the time of her commissioning on April 9, 1941, and in the action-filled years between 1941 and 1945, the *U.S.S. North Carolina* was the greatest sea weapon ever built by the United States and earned for herself a reputation that will live as long as man remembers the brutal war in the Pacific. Affectionately nicknamed "The Showboat" by Navy men, she was the first of the modern American battleships.

On June 3, 1936, Congress authorized the building of BB 55, the *U.S.S. North Carolina*. The original plans included 14-inch rifles, the maximum size allowed by the Washington Treaty. When the final plans came off the drawing board all turret fittings had been changed to house the new 16-inch rifles. On October 27, 1937, the keel was laid in Brooklyn Navy Yard. In the pre-war years, while America enjoyed the return of prosperity, the business of building the *North Carolina* moved ahead. By the time she slid down the ways on June 13, 1940, the national mood had changed considerably. A worried America watched closely when the *North Carolina*, the first battleship commissioned since 1923, joined the fleet on April 9, 1941. National publicity accompanied "The Showboat." She made history when she slid down the ways and she made history on her shakedown. She carried the first modern anti-aircraft battery, destined to down 24 Japanese planes. Her 16-inch rifles were the real show pieces when she fired the first 19-gun salvo in modern naval history. With one broadside she threw 32,750 pounds of steel at a target off Casco Bay, Maine.

When the Japanese attacked Pearl Harbor, she was relaxing in the North Atlantic. She grew up in a hurry from that time on. For the next six months, intensive training was the routine. On May 29, 1942, she put in at Hampton Roads, Virginia to load ammunition. On June 4th she stood out for the Canal Zone and on June 19th she arrived at San Pedro, California. Six days later she was on her way to war in the Pacific.

American fortunes in the Pacific were at a low ebb the summer of 1942. The ruins of the Pacific Fleet were in Pearl Harbor, and the Navy had suffered serious losses in the Java Sea campaign. The destiny of the war in the Pacific lay with the few major fighting ships, the Navy's carrier-borne air arm, the growing Amphibious Forces, the Army, and the Marine Corps. "The Showboat" was a muscular youngster among the veterans of the fleet. Could she fight? The answer wasn't long in coming. On July 15, 1942, she stood out under secret orders to Tongabatu in the Tonga Group and rendezvoused with a task force that would cover the landing of troops on a little-known island called Guadalcanal. She was ordered to screen the carriers from enemy air and surface attack. On August 24th, while steaming with the carrier *Enterprise* and an accompanying force of four cruisers and eleven destroyers, the first Japanese air attack aimed at "The Showboat" developed. When the smoke cleared, her verified score was seven enemy planes downed and many probables and assists. That was the Battle of the Eastern Solomons and it all but stripped the Japanese of carrier support.

On September 15, 1942, it happened. A Japanese torpedo tore into the battleship's armor and ripped a 100-foot gash in her side. She could still maneuver and retired to Pearl Harbor under her own power for repairs. By December 7th she was ready to fight again and resumed patrol duty in the submarine infested

Solomons. More torpedo attacks were launched at her, but none was successful. In March, 1943, she returned to Pearl Harbor to be fitted out with new and better gunnery installations, fire control, and radar gear. In the months ahead she would need every bit of modern equipment she could get.

Operation "Galvanic," the invasion of the Japanese-held Gilbert Islands, was launched from Pearl Harbor in October, 1943. "The Showboat" and the force she operated with struck hard and fast. During the next months, her gunners battered Nauru in the Gilberts, Roi and Namur in the Marshalls and, as the U.S. offensive gained momentum, she hit Truk, Guam, Saipan, Tinian, Palau, Yap, Ulithi, Woleai, Hollandia, and New Guinea. Then she raced to give Truk another pounding. "The Showboat's" seaplane pilots added another chapter to her history when they swooped into Truk Harbor to rescue downed U.S. airmen from beneath the nose of the enemy.

By June, 1944, she was a seasoned fighting veteran, and was heading into one of the most important battles of the war—the Marianas landings. She bombarded Saipan just prior to the Marine assault on June 13th. Then, six days later, her Task Force had its famous "Marianas Turkey Shoot." The Japanese struck with everything they had in a counterattack. They lost 402 planes to 17 American losses. With further Japanese air attacks on the Marianas unlikely, the fast U.S. force went after surface ships. "The Showboat" added the silhouettes of two more Japanese planes to her gun-director mounts in a sea battle that saw the destruction of two Japanese carriers and a third one damaged. On July 6, 1944, she was ordered to Bremerton, Washington, for repairs. Behind her were 25 months of warfare. After two months she stood out of Puget Sound on her way to rejoin the Pacific offensive.

She hit Leyte, Luzon, and Formosa and took part in attacks on the China Coast. She was in the assault and occupation of Iwo Jima and raided the main Japanese island of Honshu with the Fifth and Third Fleets. At Iwo Jima she emptied her entire store of ammunition on enemy installations in four days, one of the greatest naval bombardments in history. At Okinawa she hit again, and lost three men with 40 wounded.

After repairs she returned to action with the Third Fleet to strike at Japan. On August 15, 1945, her crew witnessed a strange performance. Strike planes returned early from missions over Japan and jettisoned their bomb loads just outside the formation of ships. Japan had capitulated. The war was over.

On September 5th, she anchored in Tokyo Bay; the next day, she was homeward bound. Then followed four days in Pearl Harbor, three in Panama City, one in Cristobal, and, early on the morning of October 17th, she raised Cape Cod. Four hours later she was in Boston Inner Harbor. She had won 12 battle stars, steamed 307,000 miles, entered 26 different ports, downed 24 Japanese planes, sunk a merchantman, and bombarded nine different Japanese strongholds. She had toured the war road from Guadalcanal to Tokyo Bay.

For fourteen years she swung at anchor with the mothball fleet at Bayonne, N.J. In 1960, the Navy condemned her to the scrap heap. She would be cut into scrap metal if the state of North Carolina didn't want her, but North Carolina did want her! More than 700,000 children contributed dimes, and other more affluent citizens contributed more. In less than nine months $325,000 was donated and in late September, 1961, old "Showboat" started her final voyage, this time under tow. She was moved carefully to her final berth on the Cape Fear River at Wilmington.

She is now visited by thousands. Her four engine rooms may be seen. Her decks and guns are open for inspection. On her deck, a rare restored World War II float plane, the Vought

WORLD WAR II FLOATPLANE ON THE DECK OF THE *North Carolina.*

GALLEY OF THE *U.S.S. North Carolina.*

AERIAL VIEW OF THE *U.S.S. North Carolina.*

Kingfisher, may be inspected. Every night during the summer months a sound and light spectacular entitled "The Immortal Showboat" is presented. Through the blending of the spoken word, music, unique lighting, and sound effects, plus visual effects including gunfire and explosions, her history is told in a 70-minute performance.

The Memorial is open every day of the year. In the summer months you may tour the battleship between 8 a.m. and 7:30 p.m. The ship is closed at sunset during the rest of the year.

The route through the battleship is clearly marked. Open are the ship's living space, 16-inch gun turrets, anti-aircraft guns, and the pilot house. A museum and adjoining room memorializes the names of the State's 10,000 World War II dead.

General admission is $1.00; children 6 through 11, 25 cents, and children under 5 get in free. The *U.S.S. North Carolina* is berthed in the Cape Fear River on Eagles Island in Wilmington. U.S. Highways 17, 74, and 76 lead to Wilmington.

U.S.S. Olympia.

U.S.S. OLYMPIA
Philadelphia, Pennsylvania

"You may fire when ready, Gridley." These words, spoken by Commodore George Dewey from the bridge of his flagship, *U.S.S. Olympia,* signalled the start of the Battle of Manila Bay at 5:40 a.m., May 1, 1898. As Captain C. V. Gridley, the ship's commanding officer, gave his order, an eight-inch gun from the forward turret spoke out and was joined by the rest of the guns of the American fleet. The action lasted until 12:30 p.m., resulting in the complete destruction of the enemy fleet. It was this victory of Commodore (later Admiral) Dewey's Asiatic Squadron that served notice to the world that the United States had arrived as a world power.

The *U.S.S. Olympia* was born out of a program of ships for the "New Navy" of the 1880's and 1890's. This was the program directly responsible for the rise of the steel and shipbuilding industries in the United States. She is the only remaining ship of that "New Fleet" and the last survivor of the U.S. Fleet of the Spanish-American War. She was always an outstanding ship in design and performance and was much admired both in her own country and abroad.

After the Spanish-American War, her peacetime duties included serving as flagship of the North Atlantic Squadron where she was a bulwark of strength in the protection of American lives and property in Panama, Smyrma, Turkey, and the Dominican Republic. World War I saw the *Olympia* designated Flagship of the United States Patrol Force. She served on escort and patrol duty of New York and Nova Scotia until April, 1918. Operations in European waters followed as the *Olympia* landed a force at Murmansk to preserve the peace on June 8, 1918. December, 1918, found the *Olympia* at Gibraltar, where she became Flagship of U.S. Naval Forces, Eastern Mediterranean. She served as ambassador of good will and as a symbol of strength in her many visits to ports around the Mediterranean.

A last mission brought to a close the long and honorable career of the *Olympia* when, on October 3, 1921, she sailed from Plymouth, England, to LeHavre, France, and received on board, with full military honors, the body of the Unknown Soldier for return to the United States and to his final resting place in Arlington Cemetery.

The preservation of the cruiser *Olympia* as a National Shrine and Naval Museum was made possible by an agreement between the Cruiser *Olympia* Association and the Navy Department in 1957. She was restored throughout and the original furnishings in Admiral Dewey's

quarters, the dispensary, printshop, machine shop, and barber shop can be seen again. There are exhibits including Dewey's report of the Battle of Manila Bay, contemporary newspapers, magazines, photographs, charts, and weapons of the Spanish-American War. Naval uniforms, rifles, American flags, medals, and other historical items are also on view.

The *Olympia* is 344 feet in length, has a beam of 53 feet and a displacement of 5870 tons. It has a mean draft of 21.5 feet and a maximum speed of 23 knots. Her power was twin screws, three-cylinder Triple expansion engine, 18,000 horsepower and six Scotch (Fire tube) boilers. Her complement was 34 officers and 440 men. Her armament is four eight-inch guns, 10 five-inch guns, 14 six-pounders, six one-pounders, and six 18-inch torpedo tubes.

Her berth is at Pier 11 North on the Delaware River, at the foot of Race Street in Philadelphia, Pennsylvania, close to Independence Hall. She is open from Monday through Saturday 10 a.m. to 4 p.m. and on Sundays and holidays from 11 a.m. to 4:30 p.m. She is closed on holidays and Mondays during the winter. Adults pay $1.00 to board her, children 50 cents.

THE CONTINENTAL GUNBOAT PHILADELPHIA
Smithsonian Institution, Washington, D.C.

The Continental gunboat *Philadelphia,* built and sunk on Lake Champlain in 1776, is the oldest intact man-of-war presently on exhibition in North America. Designed by Benedict Arnold as one of eight "gondolas" fitted for service in defense of the northern frontier, the *Philadelphia* was sunk at the Battle of Valcour Island in October, 1776. Today, she remains the sole survivor of that dimly remembered flotilla which frustrated Britain's first major effort to

divide and subdue her rebellious American colonies.

It was located and recovered off Valcour Island near the New York shore lying ten fathoms deep, with her mainmasts yet erect and her yards lying across the gunwales. This historic vessel evokes the memory of the hero-traitor Arnold's squadron which, though tactically annihilated, won a major strategic victory by delaying British penetration of central New

BOW VIEW OF THE *Philadelphia.*

York for nearly a year.

The near success of Arnold's thrust at Quebec on New Year's Eve and General Washington's subsequent forcing of the British evacuation of Boston in March, 1776, made the British determined to isolate New England during the following summer and fall. The Royal Governor of Canada, Sir Guy Carleton, received instructions to mount an invasion from Montreal, designed to sever New England's communications with the remaining United Colonies. There were no passable roads in northern New York, so Carleton was forced to transport his troops southward by water via the historic Lake Champlain invasion corridor. Recapture of Fort Ticonderoga, at the southern end of Lake Champlain, before the autumn of 1776, was the prime prerequisite for a successful British penetration south to Albany in the upper Hudson River Valley. The British hopes for the swift conquest of Ticonderoga were frustrated by the advance appearance of Brigadier General Arnold's Continental Army flotilla. Carleton had to spend the critical summer months at St. John's on the Richlieu River to construct a squadron powerful enough to sweep aside the American vessels. Spurred by the reports of British activity, the Continental Congress dispatched scores of shipbuilders and seamen to Skenesborough, south of Ticonderoga, to help Arnold's malaria-ravaged men build a rude fleet from nearby forests of oak, white pine, and spruce.

While the British naval commander, Captain Thomas Pringle, directed the construction of five warships, 20 gunboats, and 28 longboats, Yankee shipwrights labored to complete Arnold's flotilla of five schooners, a sloop, five galleys, and eight gondolas (gunboats).

After four weeks of provocative cruising in the upper reaches of Lake Champlain, Arnold moved south on September 23rd to Valcour Bay on the New York shore to await the British amphibious advance on Ticonderoga. On the morning of October 11th, Pringle's force, accompanied by transports for Carleton's army of British regulars, German mercenaries, and Indian allies, rounded the southern end of Valcour to discover the American squadron deployed in a rough crescent across the bay. During the six-hour engagement, stiff northerly winds hampered Pringle's heavier warships. Arnold's flagship, the 12-gun schooner *Royal Savage,* ran aground on the rock-bound southern shore of Valcour Island shortly before noon, and was subsequently burned by British boarders. The Continental battle line held firm under the superior enemy fire at a range of barely 350 yards. Arnold sustained his second loss as the riddled gondola *Philadelphia* was fatally holed by a 24-pound shot. Night permitted the Continental force to steal away, and although the Pringle force subsequently overtook the Americans, destroying them piecemeal north of Crown Point on the 13th, his own force had been heavily engaged and much of their shot expended.

Approaching Fort Ticonderoga on October 28th, as late autumn squalls swept the Lake, Carleton briefly tested the American batteries and then withdrew to St. Johns, convinced of the futility of mounting a winter siege. Arnold's brilliant delaying operations became apparent a year later with the defeat of Burgoyne's army at Saratoga in October, 1777.

It was not until 1934 that successful efforts were made to locate the remains of the squadron. Colonel Lorenzo F. Hagglund, a veteran New York salvage engineer, raised the twisted skeleton of the flagship *Royal Savage* during the summer of that year. In studying historical reports, he realized that the gunboat *Philadelphia* might also be lying on the muddy bottom of Valcour Bay. He located her and, by passing slings beneath her flat bottom, brought her to the surface on August 1, 1935, nearly 159 years after her loss off Valcour Island. After being refitted with her main battery of two 9-pounders and a 12-pounder bow gun, this historic vessel

STARBOARD QUARTER OF THE *Philadelphia.*

was exhibited on Lake Champlain for 25 years before coming to The Smithsonian Institution. She was preserved and rendered limber by an impregnation of polyethylene glycol, designed to strengthen the cellular structure of her oak timbers and planking.

She stands today in the Hall of the Armed Forces in the new Museum of History and Technology, surrounded by several hundred artifacts recovered from her resting place in Valcour Bay. Built of oak, this flat-bottomed gunboat measures some 57 feet in length and has a beam of 17 feet. She appears to have drawn no more than two feet in ballast. Fitted with a keelson but no keel, the vessel was framed with stout knees and particularly massive athwartship timbers beneath her midship gun deck. Square openings in her inner planking aft indicate that she was originally designed to mount armament on a raised quarterdeck similar to the forecastle. Her two 9-pound guns were mounted amidship and the afterdeck was employed for the accommodation of her 45 crewmen. Crude benches and

a simple hearth located forward of her port 9-pounder offer testimony to the spartan accommodations suffered by Captain Rice and his men during the autumn of 1776.

Square-rigged with a single mast, she was probably clumsy to sail and probably relied on her sweeps for additional mobility. Her two guns are believed to be of Swedish origin and antedated the gunboat by almost 100 years. Most impressive of her entire equipage is her bow gun's slide carriage, embodying the seaman's first solution to the problem of mounting heavy ordinance in men-of-war. Hurriedly constructed and armed, she bears impressive witness to the ingenuity and zeal of those Americans who fought for their independence.

The National Museum of History and Technology is on 14th Street and Constitution Avenue, N.W. in Washington, D.C. It is open in the winter from 10 a.m. to 5 p.m. The spring and summer hours are determined yearly. Admission is free.

THE PADDLEWHEELER *Rhododendron.*

THE SHOWBOAT RHODODENDRON
Clinton, Iowa

Originally launched in 1935, the coal-fired, steam towboat *Omar* was retired and turned over to the State of West Virginia in 1961. The Mountain State Centennial Commission added a third deck, built in an authentic showboat theater, redecorated and rechristened it the *Rhododendron,* and made it the focal point of the West Virginia 100th Anniversary year of 1963.

In 1966, it was acquired by the Board of Park Commissioners of Clinton, Iowa, and was towed down the Monongahela to Pittsburgh, down the Ohio to Cairo, Illinois, and up the Mississippi to her permanent mooring at the easternmost point of the great bend of the Mississippi at Clinton.

The steam-generating equipment and engines are inoperative but the boiler room and huge machinery was left intact as a museum exhibit. After six months of rebuilding, cleaning, painting, and furnishing, this paddlewheeler is now the Showboat Museum, and many relics depicting the history of life along the Mississippi are on display.

Visitors are given an opportunity to relive the days of the great riverboats when steam-driven engines, turbines, generators, and huge shafts turned the gigantic paddlewheel to furnish the source of power for the boats that plied the Mississippi.

Before the turn of the century, art and culture came to the heartland of the nation by way of the Great River. This was the golden era of the fabulous showboats that plied the Mississippi and the Ohio. The blast of the horn and the penetrating notes of the calliope heralded hours of entertainment for the people of the river towns. Melodrama, comedy, Shakespeare, minstrel shows, vaudeville—all the thrilling world of the theater unfolded in the plush, red and gold gaslight atmosphere of the showboats.

The *Rhododendron* recreates those days. It has a large and lush theater where visitors can relax and indulge in nostalgic memories of the old days. Scheduled plays are performed in the theater on weekends throughout the summer months by various college and university theater groups. The Captain's Lounge has authentic Victorian furnishings, and the Pilot's House has been restored to the last detail.

Clinton can be reached by U.S. Highway 30, the scenic route that goes through the heartlands of Iowa. The *Rhododendron* is open daily from June 1 to September 30 from 9 a.m. to 5 p.m. The admission fee for boarding is 50 cents.

THE FRIGATE ROSE
Newport, Rhode Island

The 24-gun frigate *Rose* was built at Hull, Yorkshire, in 1756, at the outbreak of the Seven Years' War with France and Spain; the well-known *H.M.S. Bounty* was later built in the same shipyard. *Rose* fought with distinction in Europe and at the capture of Martinique, St. Lucia, and Havana in 1762.

In 1768, she was chosen by James Cook for his first great voyage around the world, but at the last moment he changed his mind in favor of the merchant ship *Endeavour*. The *Rose* was sent instead to Boston, where she became the star of the so-called Pitt Packet episode. In this case, a young lawyer named John Adams launched his famous career by proving in court the illegality of impressing or drafting American seamen into the Royal Navy in peacetime.

From December, 1774 to April, 1776, *Rose* was based in Newport, Rhode Island. She was the flagship of a small squadron under the command of Commodore Sir James Wallace who had been sent to Newport to clamp down on the large-scale smuggling operations that had for years been making Rhode Island wealthy far beyond her size. The smugglers resented the intrusion and arranged to stop food being sold in the market to the fleet. When the Navy took to forcing the farmers to sell directly to the fleet, the smugglers dragged old cannons to points on the coast and fired them at the *Rose*. Wallace reacted by closing the Bay to all shipping, legal and illegal alike. As a result, Stephen Hopkins, one of the Rhode Island delegates to Congress, introduced the bill that created the American

FRIGATE *Rose* UNDER SAIL.

Navy in 1775; the first ship of that Navy to see active service was the Rhode Island sloop *Katy*, renamed *Providence* for the occasion.

When the *Rose* left Rhode Island the following April for want of food, the Rhode Island General Assembly declared Independence on May 4, 1776, two full months ahead of the rest of the country, in the hope that this would discourage Wallace from returning. In a sense, the *Rose* bears some responsibility for our actual independence.

Rose spent the next two years convoying mer-

chant ships along the American coast. In 1779, while at Savannah, Georgia, she brought news of the approach of the French invasion fleet under D'Estaing. She was ordered sunk across the channel at the mouth of the harbor. As a result, the French fleet was unable to support the Continental Army's attack, and Savannah remained in British hands until later in the War. Over the years, various pieces have been recovered in dredging operations, and some of them have been incorporated in the reconstructed *Rose*.

Rose was reconstructed in Lunenburg, Nova Scotia, in 1969, using the original plans and the few original pieces salvaged from her wreck in Georgia. *Rose* was rated as a 20- to 24-gun frigate, although she normally carried up to 32 carriage guns plus 10 swivel guns. The term "frigate" has changed meaning over the years, but in 1776 it referred to warships of 20 to 40 guns. *Rose* was considered smallish. Including the bowsprit, her length is 170 feet. The hull is 125 feet long and 31 feet wide. She draws about 13 feet of water and displaces about 500 tons. Her 13,000 square feet of dacron sails are supported by five miles of rigging, and her mainmast towers 130 feet above the water. Her original plans, together with a number of paintings of the ship, were found at the National Maritime Museum at Greenwich, England.

As you walk around the spardeck, you will notice four small cannons; these were mainly used for signalling to other ships, although in battle they could be used as anti-personnel weapons. Forward of the quarterdeck is a large hand-powered winch called a capstan; it was used for raising the anchor, hoisting sails, moving cannons, moving the ship from one dock to another, and any other heavy work to be done. The colors of the ship are authentic; most ships of this era were painted this way, including the *Constitution*.

Below decks the *Rose* contains a multitude of exhibits. Her 24 cannons, most of them ninepounders, are still fired on historic occasions. Between the cannons are over 20 models of ships of the Colonial and Revolutionary periods. The gundeck was painted red so that sailors would not panic at the sight of blood in battle.

The sailors—up to 200 of them in wartime, but only about 70 in peacetime—slept in hammocks 18 inches apart on the gundeck and the deck below. They ate on makeshift tables slung between the cannons. Also on the gundeck is the Captain's Great Cabin, authentically furnished with Queen Anne furniture. Near the

GREAT CABIN OF THE FRIGATE *Rose*.

THE FOUNDING SHIP OF THE AMERICAN NAVY, THE *Frigate Rose* IS THE ONLY REVOLUTIONARY WAR SHIP AFLOAT.

Captain's Cabin are 15 mannequins clothed in reproductions of uniforms of naval and marine officers in the American, British, and French forces at the time of the Revolution.

The *Rose's* figurehead is a growling lion measuring over nine feet tall. The *Rose* has been under sail many times in recent years. She can be visited at King's Dock, just off America's Cup Avenue in Newport, Rhode Island. She is open daily from April to December from 10 a.m. to sunset. Admission is $1 for adults and 75 cents for children 6 to 12 years old.

THE *Sherman Zwicker*.

THE SHERMAN ZWICKER
GRAND BANKS SCHOONER MUSEUM
Boothbay Harbor, Maine

The Grand Banks of the North Atlantic Ocean figured heavily in the exploration of the New World. Fishing boats from Europe came to the Grand Banks long before Columbus sailed for the West Indies. It is also believed that the English used various Newfoundland coves and inlets as a base for their fishing operations, while the French used the Cape Breton area of Nova Scotia.

The Banks are part of an underwater plateau of sand which follows the eastern shore of New England, Nova Scotia, and Newfoundland. The Grand Banks, one of the world's most productive fishing areas, are located off the southeast coast of Newfoundland and cover an area of over 35,000 square miles.

In the past, fishing vessels would make about three trips each year to the Grand Banks to get their catch of cod and return to their various home ports in New England and the Maritime Provinces of Canada. The *Sherman Zwicker* was part of that fishing fleet. The trips would last from six weeks to three months depending on weather and fishing conditions.

Today large, modern refrigerated fishing vessels make speedy trips to the Grand Banks from various ports. In the early days all the fish caught on the Banks had to be salted in order to preserve them for the return voyage to market.

Life aboard the *Sherman Zwicker* was strenuous. The crewmen put in long days. Work started by 2:00 a.m. They baited their mile and and a half length of line on hooks fastened every ten feet apart on a three-foot section of twine. Each line had identifying kegs at each end. After the lines were set out in the water they were tended by men in dories three or four times a day: before and after breakfast, after dinner, and just before supper. The trawl line was brought over the gunwale by a man standing in the bow, who would pass the line back to the second man in the stern, who would remove the fish, place them in a tub, and rebait the hooks. After tending their trawl, the men would row back to the schooner where the fish would be cleaned and prepared for salting. This routine would continue until the vessel's hold was filled with cod fish, and it would then start its trip back to the home port.

It was not until the middle of the last century that the famous Banks fishing industry of Lunenberg had its beginnings. The Zwicker firm was founded in 1789, and was the first to fit out vessels for this enterprise. At the time of her launching in March of 1942, the *Sherman Zwicker* was Nova Scotia's largest fishing vessel, measuring: length, 142 feet; beam, 26 feet; hold, 11 feet, 6 inches; engines, Fairbanks Morse, 320 horsepower. She was launched from the Smith and Rhuland Shipyards in Lunenberg, Nova Scotia.

Each year the *Sherman Zwicker* would usually make three trips to the Banks: early March, May and June, and mid-September. During the fall and winter she made several trips to South America, carrying a cargo of fish down and returning with a hold full of salt.

For nearly twenty years the *Sherman Zwicker* sailed from the port of Lunenberg with her crew of 28 men for the fishing grounds under the command of Captain Crouse, after which time she was sold to Captain Maxwell Burry of Glovertown, Newfoundland, who used the vessel to service the codfish fisheries on the coast of Labrador. Her last trip to Labrador was made in 1968. It was then that the schooner was retired from active fishing and opened to the public as a maritime museum in Boothbay Harbor, Maine.

The schooner is not as colorful a ship as some of her sisterships, but is typical of her class. She is known as a dory schooner and a salt banker, since the men fished from dories and the fish brought back to port were preserved in salt. Cleaning and preparing the fish was done on the deck, where there are hand pumps, the large winch used to raise the anchor, and the various other smaller tools of the fishing industry. The six maroon-colored dories are all stacked on the port side, and the six buff-colored on the starboard side. The difference in color would tell the Captain on which side to raise a dory back on board.

The wheel is located at the stern of the ship. It was placed over the rudder to facilitate the mechanical steering mechanism. Most early Grand Bank schooners had no wheelhouse and the helmsman would stand out in the open weather when on watch. In the *Sherman Zwicker's* wheelhouse are the compass, radio direction finder, and the radar.

About one-third of the crew slept in the Main Cabin which also contained the sleeping quarters for the captain in a separate compartment. The Captain's cabin contains electronic gear used in navigation. The Engine Room is filled with the massive Fairbanks Morse, 320 horsepower engine which drove the ship at a cruising speed of 9½ knots. The engine has no reverse gear and is hooked directly to the drive shaft and the propeller. The engine is still in good running condition and is used to propel the ship to drydock each year. On the port wall are the ends of three large air tanks. The compressed air is used to roll the engine over for starting and also for blowing the ship's horn in foggy weather. On the starboard wall is a Lister auxiliary engine used for pumping water, compressing air, and generating electricity.

A passageway into and out of the Fish Hold and into the Forecastle was recently cut into the bulkheads for the passage of visitors. The Hold has a capacity of 320,000 pounds of fish. The bins on both sides were to stop the load from shifting in rough weather. The Forecastle in the bow contains the sleeping quarters of the crew. It also holds the galley with its large cook stove and the various food lockers. The Forecastle was the recreation area for the fishermen during the evenings.

Boothbay Harbor can be reached by U.S. 1 and into Route 27. The Schooner Museum is located on Commercial Street. It is open daily from 9 a.m. to 9 p.m. The admission fee is $1; children under 12 years of age, 50 cents.

W. P. SNYDER, JR.
Marietta, Ohio

When the sternwheeler *W. P. Snyder, Jr.* arrived on the Muskingum River in September, 1955, she resigned her position as workhorse of the river system to become a public museum, honoring the once proud fleet of steamboats which brought prosperity and a good dash of romantic adventure to the American heartland.

The sternwheel steamboat, like the steam locomotive, has passed from the American scene, both being replaced by the more efficient diesel engine. In 1945, half of the boats on the Mississippi River system were still steam-powered; today, the great diesel towboat fleet numbers well over 1000.

The steamboat began its nearly century and one half of service on the inland rivers in 1811, when the *New Orleans*, built in Pittsburgh by the Ohio Steam Boat Navigation Company, made its maiden voyage to Cincinnati, Louisville, and on to New Orleans. Ten years later there were about 75 steamboats on the Mississippi, and after three decades there were 450 boats in operation.

The arrival of the steamboat brought a boom to the towns along the western waters, which were already enjoying a prosperous trade by flatboat and keelboat. Steamboat arrivals at Cincinnati reached 360 in 1825, 1000 in 1829, and mounted to 4000 in 1848. "Steam navigation has colonized the West," wrote a contemporary in 1841. It brought the western territory nearer to the east by nine-tenths of the distance. It advanced the history of national colonization and national production by at least a century.

The heyday of the steamboat was the 20-year period from 1845 to the end of the Civil War. Hundreds of sidewheelers and a number of sternwheelers, ranging from small "short traders" of under 100 tons to the 350-foot, 1115-ton "floating palace" *Eclipse*, carried freight and passengers on the western river system. The rumble of the railroad and the end of the Civil War saw the decline of the great packets and freight boats.

A renewal of life came to the rivers with the construction of dams and canals throughout

THE STERNWHEELER *W.P. Snyder, Jr.*

the system. The new era was dominated by towboat and barge, transporting thousands of tons of oil, coal, ore, chemicals, etc. The demands of this new traffic soon brought the replacement of the steam sternwheel towboat by the diesel-propelled craft.

The *W. P. Snyder, Jr.* is the descendant of a long line of sternwheelers and towboats. For more than fifty years the more easily maneuverable and faster sidewheelers ruled the river. With the development of steam boilers and higher steam pressures, and improvements in boat construction, the sternwheelers came into their own after 1870, and by 1880 they outnumbered the sidewheelers three to one.

The *W. P. Snyder, Jr.* was born the *W. H. Clingerman* in 1918. Built by the firm of James Rees & Sons Co., Pittsburgh, for the Carnegie Steel Co., she was used primarily to bring coal from the mines along the upper Monongahela River to the Carnegie works downriver at Clair-

ton, though she also pushed steel tows and once made a trip as far south as Memphis. In 1938, Carnegie renamed the boat the *J. L. Perry*. In the fall of 1945, the Crucible Steel Co. gave her her present name. As the *W. P. Snyder, Jr.* she was finally retired in good condition.

Mounted on a steel hull, she is 175 feet long and 32.3 feet wide and has a paddlewheel 21 feet in diameter on the stern. On the river she is known as a "poolboat," since her pilothouse is set forward on the second deck, rather than on the roof. This was done to enable her to operate under the low bridges on the Monongahela. The boat is equipped with two sets of compound engines which generate 750 horsepower. Each engine has a high pressure cylinder 14 inches in diameter, a low pressure cylinder 28 inches in diameter, and a common piston stroke of seven feet. The exhausted steam from the low pressure cylinders is carried into a surface condenser and pumped from there into the boilers. The

boiler plant consists of four "western river boilers," each 28 feet long and 40 inches in diameter. In each boiler are two 15-inch flues through which the flame, having passed under the boilers from the flame bed, returns forward and is piped into the smokestacks. The boiler fuel is bituminous coal, fed to the fireboxes by automatic stokers.

Although the *W. P. Snyder, Jr.* incorporated the improvements of its day, many of the characteristics of her nineteenth-century predecessors were retained. There is the elaborate "hog chain" support: a system of steel cables, mounted on posts, stretching along the sides of the boat to keep it from "hogging," or buckling in the center, and to help carry the weight of the paddlewheel; there is the orthodox pilotwheel, now only for emergency use in case the automatic steering apparatus fails; there is the bell signal system from the pilothouse to the engine room identical to that of Mark Twain's day. The stateroom and cabin construction are just as they were on river boats a century ago.

The *W. P. Snyder, Jr.* was given to the State of Ohio by the Crucible Steel Company of America. It is administered as a section of the River Museum of the Campus Martius State Memorial. The River Museum displays scale models, oil paintings, photographs, whistles, and other mementoes of river boats of the past and present. Its permanent mooring is in the Muskingum River at Marietta, Ohio.

The Campus Martius Museum is located on the corner of Washington and Second Streets in Marietta, Ohio. The *W. P. Snyder, Jr.* is docked on the Muskingum River at Sacra Via near Front Street in Marietta. The facilities are open to the public without charge from 9 a.m. to 5 p.m. Mondays through Saturdays, 1 p.m. to 5 p.m. Sundays.

THE *Star of India.*

STAR OF INDIA
San Diego, California

Originally, the *Star of India* was the British full-rigged ship *Euterpe,* launched at Ramsey, Isle of Man, on November 14, 1863. She is the oldest merchant vessel afloat today. She was heavily built, for iron ships were new then and they were built well in those pre-welding, pre-airhammer days. Every one of those hundreds of thousands of rivets were driven by hand and, in 1863, the underwriters demanded very heavy plates, since they were distrustful of ships which were not built of wood. All that extra metal paid off, for despite years of neglect, the *Star of India* is still afloat.

She has been through a lot since that autumn afternoon of her launching; many times disaster was close—from ice, from mountainous seas, from rocks, and from neglect. She's been dismasted off Trincomalee and set on fire in Liverpool; she has known mutiny and sudden death, and ice almost carried her to her doom on the rocky shore of the Alaskan Peninsula.

She got off to a bad start. Hours out of Liverpool on her maiden voyage she collided with a Spanish brig; her head-rigging was badly damaged, and her crew mutinied. She refitted and went on to India. On the next voyage, a hurricane caught her off Madras and her masts and rigging went over the side. They patched her up and sailed her to Calcutta for refitting. Ten days out on the homeward voyage her master died and the mate brought her home. At different times she just missed an iceberg, her spars let go, her steering wheel was smashed by a heavy sea, a man fell from aloft, and on the long, dismal voyages out from England, emigrants died and babies were born.

The opening of the Suez Canal doomed the long-range colonial trader. Steamers could now make it to India economically. Her long time owners sold her to J. J. Moore of San Francisco and she was placed under Hawaiian registry. She operated in the export timber trade out of Puget Sound for Australia. At the turn of the century she was picked up by the Alaska Packers Association of San Francisco and joined their fleet of four beautiful ships. *Euterpe* became the *Star of India.* So that she might be handled by a smaller crew, the Packers cut down her rig from full-rigged ship to bark. Yards were removed from her mizzenmast and replaced by fore-and-aft canvas. They also built a long extension onto her poop to provide quarters for fishermen. From 1902 until 1923, she went from San Francisco to Bristol Bay, Alaska, every April, with tin plate, box-shook, oil, and other necessities for the salmon canneries—and as many as 250 fishermen and cannery hands. Late each summer she came back through the Golden Gate with a full load of canned salmon.

Time ran out for square-riggers in the Alaskan fisheries. One by one her sister ships in the fleet were sold. Some went into the movies, some were cut down to barges, and some were scrapped. The only lucky ones were *Star of Alaska* (now San Francisco's famed museum-ship *Balclutha*) and *Star of India*. In 1926, she was bought by the late James Wood Coffroth, who gave her to the Zoological Society of San Diego; the idea was to make her into a floating aquarium and museum. The Great Depression scotched those plans and she was left to gather rust, dry rot, and scaling paint—in short, she became a denizen of a maritime Skid Row. San Diego called her "that old tub" and zealous patriots wanted her cut up for scrap to aid the war effort—or turned over to the Navy for use as a target ship!

In 1957, when she was at her lowest point, Captain Alan Villiers, noted author and lecturer and former square-rigger officer, came to San Diego to examine the old ship. In the press, he pulled no punches in expressing his opinion of the kind of community which would let such a thing happen to such a grand old lady of the sea. It stung people to action and a Restoration Committee was formed. It took a long time to raise funds.

It took almost longer to restore her. The extra thickness of her bottom plates had saved her. She was sandblasted, painted, and towed to a berth at the Embarcadero. The almost Herculean job of restoration began. Financial crisis followed financial crisis, loans were floated, arms twisted, and doorbells rung. Congress gave $23,000 to compensate for damage done when she was dismantled as a wartime measure. She began to shape up. The long, ugly poop-extension was ripped away. The tongue-and-groove bulkhead of pine boards was replaced by hardwood panelling as it had been when she was in the colonial trade. The strengthened masts were lowered into place by a huge crane, and one by one the lower yards were crossed. Topmasts, topgallantmasts, and upper yards, however, were sent up in the traditional sea-going style with the power supplied by a half-dozen devoted volunteers. A lot of welding, carpentry, chipping, and burning was done. With only some $800 left from the fund, it was reluctantly decided to open her to the public at an admission charge, although she was far from complete. The reaction was and still is favorable. Captain Villiers came back to San Diego for her 100th birthday and the ship swarmed with guests, the press, and television crews. She was officially christened *Star of India*. To this date restoration still goes on. A tired old hulk does not become a well-kept museum ship overnight, but she is well worth visiting and admiring.

The *Star of India's* length on waterline is 205 feet. Her beam is 35 feet, the depth of her hold 23 feet, 6 inches. Her mainmast from deck to truck is 124 feet, 8 inches; her main yard, 72 feet. Her jibboom is 55 feet and her tonnage is 1197.

The ship is berthed at Harbor Drive between Ash and Market Streets in San Diego. She is open to the public daily from 9 a.m. to 8 p.m. The admission charge is $1 for adults and 25 cents for children.

THE *Star of India*, FROM A PAINTING BY CAPT. KENNETH D. REYNARD.

THE *U.S.S. Texas* SAILING THROUGH THE PANAMA CANAL IN 1919.

THE U.S.S. TEXAS
San Jacinto Battleground, Texas

When the *U.S.S. Texas* came home to start an honorable retirement as a living musuem, she was a 34-year-old veteran of two World Wars. Her retirement date was April 21, 1948.

She was commissioned in 1914, saw action with the Sixth Battle Squadron in World War I, and carried the name of her state into battle from the shores of Normandy to the beaches of Okinawa in World War II.

The story of "Old T," as she was familiarly called, began with commissioning ceremonies at the Norfolk Navy Yard on March 12, 1914. Hailed as the pride of the fleet, the *Texas* was a two-stacked, cage-masted triumph of naval architecture. Her twin-gunned, 14-inch turrets were of the latest design and she was reputed to have the largest and most efficient set of engines afloat.

She joined the fleet on her maiden voyage without benefit of a shakedown run. But while "Old T" shook down with the fleet, she fulfilled all requirements of the Navy Department. She joined the Grand Fleet as a unit of the Sixth Battle Squadron on January 30, 1918, and on her fifth day out fired the first shot of her career. The Grand Fleet was at sea to hunt down the German Fleet on a rumor that it had put out to sea.

In April, 1941, the "T" started preparing for another war and shortly after began the long and tedious neutrality patrols across the stormy North Atlantic, into the German-declared war zone. Her guns fully manned, the "T" was ready for instant action six months before the United States entered the war.

December 7, 1941, found the *Texas* in the harbor of Portland, Maine, taking for herself and her crew a well-deserved "shore leave" after months of arduous patrol duty. Quickly loaded with provisions and ammunition, she was soon readied for the role she was to play in World War II. By this time the "Old Lady" did not expect a starring role in the "big show," but her presence was forcibly felt in every theater of action during the long war. She was at Casablanca, Gibraltar, Morocco, Normandy, Iwo Jima, and, finally, Okinawa.

Off the shores of North Africa she poured her 14-inch projectiles into ammunition dumps and armed columns moving up to the aid of the enemy. On June 6, 1944, her dawn bombardment hurled 250 projectiles into coastal defense batteries, demolishing the lethal 155mm installations and paving the way for the invasion forces. At Cherbourg, in company with the *Nevada, Arkansas,* and a small cruiser force, she engaged other coastal batteries. It was at Cherbourg, during a gun duel with the German Navy, that the *Texas* was tagged by the enemy for the first time, hit by two 288mm projectiles. One struck the top of the conning tower and exploded, wiping out the navigation bridge, killing one man, and injuring 13 others. The other projectile was a dud.

Her wounds healed, the "T" was dispatched to the other side of the world to join a mighty armada under Admiral Nimitz—the Pacific Fleet. At Iwo Jima, she blasted enemy installations on Mount Suribachi. Her crew witnessed the now-famous flag raising and then steamed on to participate in the invasion of Okinawa. The crew which brought the *Texas* through the most gruelling naval operation in history brought her home after V. J. Day to receive a grateful "well done" from the nation she had served so well.

Long past the retirement age for battlewagons, the heroine of two wars seemed doomed for oblivion and possible destruction. But the people of Texas created a Battleship *Texas* Commission for the purpose of establishing the "Old T" as a shrine. Today, the *Texas* is permanently moored at her final resting place in the still, shallow waters beside the towering San Jacinto Monument.

THE *U.S.S. Texas*, REFITTED, IN THE CANAL IN 1929.

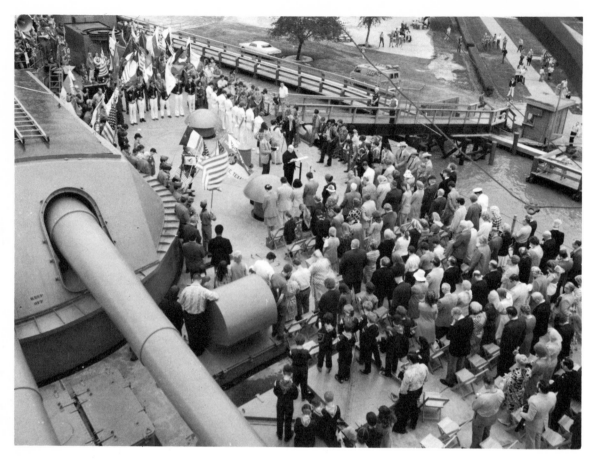

CEREMONIES ON BOARD THE *Texas*.

The *Texas* was the last major fighting ship to use reciprocating engines; all subsequent ships used the more efficient and less space-consuming turbines. Before her major transformation, she was primarily a coal burner, with oil as an auxiliary fuel in case of emergency. The electric generating capacity of 1200 kilowatts was sufficient to serve a good sized community. She used about half of this power, with balance as standby. Before her transformation, all the deck machinery fans and rudders were powered by small steam engines; later, all of this was done by electricity from her generators.

She is 573 feet in overall length, and her extreme breadth is 106 feet. Her height at top foremast is 138 feet; her draft is 28 feet, 6 inches. Her tonnage is 35,000 and her horsepower 27,000. She had a peacetime complement of 1625 crew, 100 officers, and 85 Marines. She traveled 121,000 miles in action against the enemy and was 478 days in actual operation against the enemy.

The *U.S.S. Texas* rests on the bottom of the slip dredged for her, and is reached from land by a bridge, as she is surrounded by water. She is moored next to the San Jacinto Monument, and can be reached from Houston by Interstate Highway 10. Admission hours are daily from 12 to 6 p.m. Adults pay $1 admission, children from 6 to 11 pay 50 cents.

THE *Texas* AT PERMANENT BERTH, SAN JACINTO BATTLE MONUMENT.

THE *Ticonderoga* IN PERMANENT MOORING NEAR LIGHTHOUSE.

S.S. TICONDEROGA

Shelburne Museum,
Shelburne, Vermont

The Shelburne Museum is the owner of the *Ticonderoga*, the finest remaining example of the once dominant North American type of steamboat. This vessel, 220 feet in length and 59 feet in beam, with a displacement of 892 tons, is the last of a long line on Lake Champlain, which has known the steamboat longer than any other lake in the world. The first sidewheeler, the *Vermont*, was launched in 1808, only one year after the first journey of the *Clermont*. Ninety-eight years later, in 1906, the *Ticonderoga* slid from the ways in Shelburne Harbor to begin a 47-year career in the freight, passenger, and excursion business. In early days she and her companion ships, the *Vermont III* and *Chateaugay*, made a fortune for her owners, the Champlain Transportation Company, but her revenue had so dwindled by 1950 that she was slated to follow her forebears to the scrap pile that spring.

In the winter of 1951, following a money-raising, dock-building, and publicity campaign to "Save the TI," she was purchased by the Shelburne Museum which undertook to continue her in operation. She ran three years, flying the flag of the Shelburne Museum, as a traveling museum of steamboating, carrying to the corners of Lake Champlain tens of thousands of excursionists from all parts of the country. In the fall of 1953, as the result of a lack of personnel qualified to run a vessel of a type which is all but extinct, the *Ticonderoga* was placed in retirement.

She served long and well, carrying over a million people and perhaps several times that many tons of freight in a total journey on Lake Champlain equivalent to some fifty trips around the world. She called at every port on Lake Champlain except Rouses Point and Whitehall and carried a roster of famous people, including several Presidents of the United States. In her first daily schedule between Westport, New York, and St. Alban's Bay, Vermont, she hauled quantities of freight, including horses, cows, sheep, apples, butter, and dry goods. In the evenings she doubled as an excursion boat for crowds of up to 1200 persons. She might not have survived World War II had it not been for gasoline rationing. When she returned to line run between the lake ports, stranded motorists swarmed to her decks by the thousands.

The *Ticonderoga* is the last surviving sidewheel steamboat to have been built in the grand and unique American tradition. The interiors of her dining room, recess, and stateroom hall are paneled in butternut and cherry, with gold stenciling on the ceilings. Originally, she called for a crew of some 29 persons, including captain, two pilots, two engineers, two mates, four firemen, purser, freight clerk, stewardess, hall and recess boys, and 15 deckhands, cooks, and waiters. Her vertical steam engine, a handmade product of the famous Fletcher Engine Company, extends upward through three decks to the picturesque walking beam, one end of which is fastened to an immense connecting rod that turns the paddlewheels, and the other to the piston of the 53-inch cylinder. Powered by two boilers consuming a ton of coal an hour, and capable of a speed of

18 miles an hour, the engine is similar to that invented by Thomas Newcomen, who, in 1705, designed a "walking beam" engine for pumping water out of British coal mines.

For a year the trustees of the Shelburne Museum deliberated over plans to preserve this fine specimen of marine architecture. She couldn't be properly maintained at her winter mooring with the ice pressing upon her hull, nor would she be accessible to the public far from the Museum grounds. They decided on the incredible scheme of moving her, intact, 9000 feet overland to the Museum. They decided that she would also fit in with the group of early Vermont buildings without causing any aesthetic shock.

It took six months to get her moved into her present location. It was necessary to raise the boat from lake level onto a special steel cradle which straddled flat cars on two sets of railroad tracks. In this manner, she journeyed down highways, under high tension wires and telephone lines, through a swamp, a patch of woods, barnyards, cornfields, and railroad tracks until in April, 1955, she reached her permanent mooring near the lighthouse on the Museum grounds.

The Shelburne Museum is on U.S. Highway 7 in Shelburne, Vermont. It is open daily from May 15th to October 15th and on holidays from 9 a.m. to 5 p.m. Museum admission is $3.50 for adults, $1.50 for children.

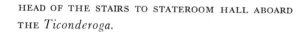

HEAD OF THE STAIRS TO STATEROOM HALL ABOARD THE *Ticonderoga.*

JULIUS C. WILKIE
Winona, Minnesota

THE *Julius C. Wilkie.*

The *Julius C. Wilkie* is a sternwheel steamboat that was built in 1898 and is now a museum boat on display to the public at the river bank of Winona. It is one of the few original paddlewheelers still preserved and on display on the Mississippi.

The Mississippi River system is bordered by one-third of the United States, and America's industrial past is inextricably tied to the Mother of Waters. For over a century the steamboats that dominated life along the river and its tributaries played a leading role in one of the most exciting chapters of America's history. They were the prime agents responsible for the settling and expansion of the great Middle West and formed the principal link between the new settlers and the rest of the world.

In its day steamboating was a hazardous service. Riverbanks caved in and channels changed. It took an intricate knowledge of the ever-changing waterways to navigate safely. The chance that the riverboat boiler might explode was a constant danger. The possibility of the boat being grounded on a sand bar, or of ripping its hull on a snag or sawyer and being sent to join the long list of paddlewheelers lining the bottom of the Mississippi, was ever-present.

Despite all the hazards and hardships, the deep-throated whistle of the steamboat was an irresistible siren's song for all restless souls who wanted to travel, not to mention industrial concerns who were able to ship their goods cheaply on the river. A floating ton requires less energy to keep it moving on water than any other known form of transportation, and the rivers are a free passageway.

Now that the smokeless and unromantic diesel has replaced the coal-fired stern and sidewheel paddlers of the all-wood-hulled steamboat era, it is imperative that we preserve some of those veteran boats to recall the drama of river life of not so long ago. The *Julius C. Wilkie*, built in 1898 at the Kahlke Brothers' boatyard in Rock Island, Illinois, was the next to last of the steamboats to ply the Upper Mississippi. It provided 56 years of service before being docked in its new berth as a steamboat museum. Weighing 62 tons, it has all the equipment of its steamboat era ranging from the picturesque paddlewheel and maze of machinery below decks to its calliope on the top deck. It has room for a crew of 12. The *Julius C. Wilkie* measures 96 feet in length, has a 24-foot beam, and drew four feet of water. She was powered by two engines, steam driven from twin coal hand-fired boilers, and they delivered 200 horsepower to drive the 18-foot paddlewheel. The boilers carried 184 pounds of steam pressure and are 30 feet long.

There is an original Tangley Calliope in back of the wheelhouse. On exhibition are models of various types of steamboats, photographs, and navigational instruments that recall the early days of steamboat traffic through Winona.

The *Julius C. Wilkie* is moored in Levee Park at the head of Main Street in Winona. U.S. Highways 14 and 61 run through Winona. The boat may be visited from May 1st to September 30th, Monday through Saturday from 9 a.m. to 5 p.m., Sundays and holidays from 10 a.m. to 6 p.m. Adults pay $1 admission; students, 50 cents; and children under 12, 25 cents.

THE 1ST SIX FRIGATES of THE U.S. NAVY

① UNITED STATES (1797–1866) LAUNCHED, MAY 10, 1797 (44 GUNS)
② CONSTELLATION (1797–1847 / 1854–2018) Ⓛ SEPT. 7, 1797 (38)
③ CONSTITUTION (1797–1881 / 1906–2018) Ⓛ OCT. 21, 1797 (44)
④ CONGRESS (1799–1834) Ⓛ APR. 1, 1799 (38)
⑤ CHESAPEAKE (1799–1819?) Ⓛ JUN. 20, 1799 (38)
⑥ PRESIDENT (1800–1817?) Ⓛ APR. 10, 1800 (44)

MARITIME MUSEUMS

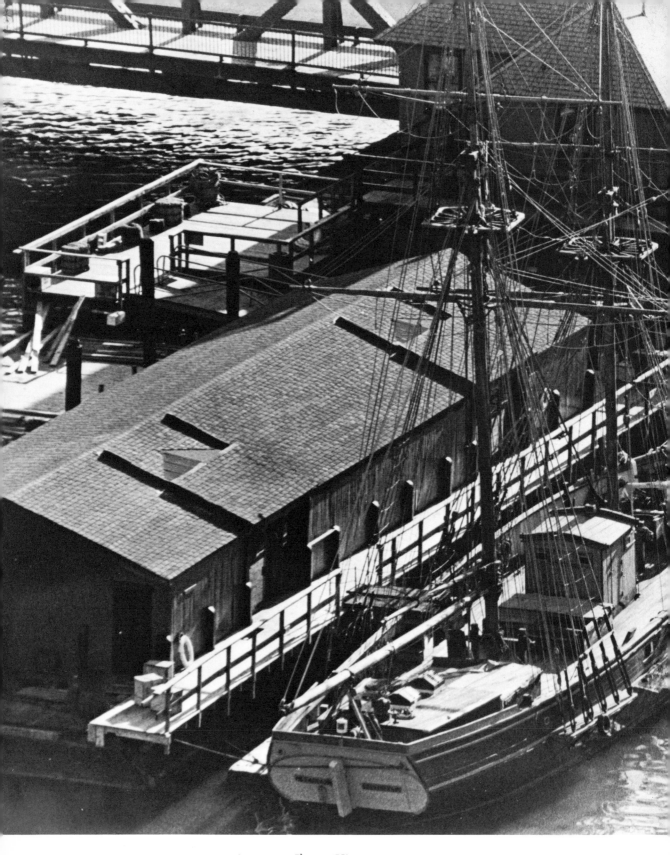

THE BOSTON TEA PARTY SHIP (THE BRIG *Beaver II*) AND MUSEUM.

BOSTON TEA PARTY
SHIP AND MUSEUM

Boston, Massachusetts

Brig Beaver II

On the night of December 16, 1773, a small band of Bostonians climbed aboard three vessels moored at Griffin's Wharf and destroyed 340 chests of dutied tea by dumping it into the harbor. This violent protest of Parliament's tax on tea—the Boston Tea Party—shattered a three-year period of relative calm between Great Britain and her colonies. Almost without interruption, the violence led to the outbreak of war at Lexington and Concord.

Boston had long been regarded as a trouble spot by the British authorities. Royal governors had complained for years that a motley crowd of inhabitants ruled the town with no respect for their "betters." Previously, British troops sent there to keep order had found it necessary to open fire on a mob in what became known as the Boston Massacre. In the fall of 1773, when the East India Company sent cargoes of surplus tea to four American ports, it was only at Boston that the shipment was destroyed.

Upon learning of the Boston Tea Party, the British ministry decided the time had come to punish the insurrectionists. The port was closed to all shipping, more troops were sent and stationed there under a military governor, and the colony's charter was revised. The news of these "Coercive Acts" created a wave of sympathy for Boston throughout America. If Parliament could close Boston Harbor and change the charter of Massachusetts Bay, then the same things could happen to the other colonies, and Boston's cause became the cause of all the colonies.

Patriot leaders called a Congress at Philadelphia in September, 1774, to consider their course of action. There it was decided to establish a total boycott of British goods, enforced by local

RARE TEA CHEST IN THE MUSEUM.

committees of inspection, until Parliament would repeal the "Coercive Acts."

Boston had become an armed camp, with British troops garrisoning the city and patriot minutemen preparing for war in the surrounding towns. On the night of April 18, 1775, a British expedition set out from Boston to seize American military stores. The next morning, fighting broke out between the British troops and the minutemen, first at Lexington and then at Concord. The American Revolution had begun!

The brig *Beaver II*, a full-size working replica of one of the three ships involved in the Boston Tea Party, is the focus of the permanent exhibit dramatizing Boston's most famous historical event. It is a 112-foot brigantine, constructed in Denmark and sailed from England to Boston with a cargo of tea during the summer of 1973. No plans of the original tea ships exist, so an exact reproduction of the *Beaver* was impossible to create. The hull of an old Danish trading schooner was discovered, the tonnage and dimensions of which were similar to those of the original *Beaver*, as taken from Lloyd's registry of 1773. The *Beaver II* was rebuilt from the hull up according to the plans of William Avery Baker, nautical advisor to the Boston Tea Party Ship and Museum.

The *Beaver II* measures 112 feet, including her booms. The actual deck length is 76 feet with a breadth of 22 feet. Her two masts of Douglas Fir extend 72 and 64 feet from the deck of the ship. There are almost 10 miles of line on the brig, most involved in the extremely intricate sail plan. It is restored to show a typical eighteenth-century cookhouse, crew's quarters, and captan's cabin.

Beaver II is located on a floating barge immediately adjacent to the Tea Party Museum. The Museum tells the dramatic story of the Boston Tea Party and features two slide shows. It also has a series of standing panels incorporating descriptive materials and historical documents that portray the broader story of the pre-revolutionary era, placing the Boston Tea Party in its historical perspective. There is also a relief map of eighteenth-century Boston tracing the route of the Tea Party participants. A rare eighteenth-century tea chest, reputed to have been among those hurled overboard during the Tea Party, is also exhibited. It belonged to Jaazaniah Crosby, a Massachusetts patriot who allegedly plucked the chest from the harbor after the Tea Party. It was in the possession of the Crosby family for generations and is on loan to the Museum.

The *Beaver II* is permanently moored at the official Tea Party site at the Congress Street Bridge in the Fort Point Channel in Boston. It is open every day from 9 a.m. to 7 p.m. The admission fees are $1.50 for adults and 75 cents for children. It is open all year round except for Thanksgiving, Christmas, and New Year's Day.

THE *Edna E. Lockwood.*

THE OYSTER
SLOOP *Lenard*.

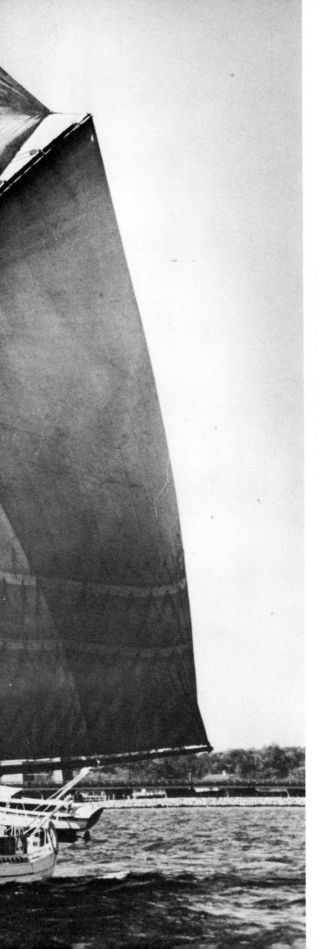

CHESAPEAKE BAY MARITIME MUSEUM

St. Michaels, Maryland
Lenard and *Lockwood*

Located in an old shipbuilding center and battle site of the War of 1812, the Chesapeake Bay Maritime Museum has moored to the Museum's piers two vessels that are retired from the oyster dredging trade and preserved as dockside exhibits.

The *Lenard* is the last surviving round-bottomed, gaff-rigged oyster sloop. She was built in 1882 at Taylor's Island, Maryland. She is 45 feet long, has a beam of 16.6 feet and a 2.8 foot draft with centerboard up. In addition to the two lowers and the topsail she carried a flying jib on occasion.

The *Lockwood* is the last "chunk-built" bugeye with the original rig left on Chesapeake Bay. She is not framed and planked in the conventional way, but has an underbody made of nine big logs, carved and fitted like those of a log canoe. She was built at Tilghman Island, Maryland, in 1889. She is 53.6 feet long, has a 15.9 foot beam, and a 2.7 foot draft with board up.

Both of these vessels were retired from the oyster trade about 1966. They are not now taken out under sail but are moored to the Museum piers where visitors are permitted to go on board the *Lenard*. After repairs on the *Lockwood* are completed, visitors will be permitted to board her also.

The Maritime Museum can be reached on Maryland State Highway 33. It is on Chesapeake Bay. In the winter it is open from Tuesday to Sunday, including holidays, from 10 a.m. to 4 p.m. In the summer it is open daily from 10 a.m. to 5 p.m. Adults pay $1.50 admission; children from 6 to 16 pay 50 cents.

FULL-SCALE REPLICAS OF THE THREE SHIPS WHICH BROUGHT THE FIRST ENGLISH SETTLERS TO JAMES-TOWN. THE *Susan Constant, Godspeed,* AND *Discovery* MAY BE SEEN AT FESTIVAL PARK. VISITORS ARE ALLOWED ABOARD THE *Susan Constant.*

JAMESTOWN FOUNDATION
Jamestown, Virginia
Susan Constant II, Godspeed II, and *Discovery*

On December 20, 1606, three square-rigged merchant ships, the *Susan Constant,* the *Godspeed,* and the *Discovery,* manned by 39 crewmen, sailed from Blackwall, England, carrying 144 soldiers, gentlemen, craftsmen, and laborers to Virginia. The ships were not greatly different from the Roman galleys of Nero's day, one thousand years earlier. Park Rouse, Jr., Director of the Jamestown Foundation, writes, "Through the Dark and Middle Ages, Europe had clung to the belief that a seagoing ship should be shaped like a whale. Like the metal armor the settlers brought with them, their cumbersome ships were a remnant of medievalism in the modern world."

The Jamestown ships were inspired by merchantmen which cruised the waters of the Mediterranean for a thousand years after the birth of Christ. When the English Crusaders visited the Holy Land in the twelfth century, they took home to England these ideas to superimpose on their own small fore-and-aft rigged vessels. Spanish vessels, taken as prizes by Sir Francis Drake from the Spanish Armada in 1588, were models for English ships to come.

The Jamestown ships, like the Mediterranean ships that inspired their design, had deep draft and immense weight which gave stability for ocean crossings. Their virtue and strength lay in their broad beams and heavy timbers.

Sailing the West Indies route, they reached the Virginia coast on April 26th, planted a cross at Cape Henry on April 29th, anchored at Point Comfort on April 30th, and finally arrived at Jamestown Island on May 13, 1607, landing the following morning on a site since washed away.

About the voyage, Park Rouse wonders, "How could three sailing ships of different size and speed have kept together on so long an ocean voyage!" The voyage took four and one half months. He suggests, "perhaps the 100-ton *Susan Constant* towed the 20-ton *Discovery* and thus enabled the 40-ton *Godspeed* to keep pace. . . . No doubt the little ships were helped in staying together at night by means of a burning cresset torch on the stern of the lead ship, the *Susan Constant*, commanded by Captain Christopher Newport. Whatever the case, the crews showed superb seamanship in crossing relatively uncharted waters together with no loss of life."

The nineteenth-century British political scientist Lord Bryce wrote: "The landing at Jamestown was one of the great events in the history of the world—an event to be compared for its momentous consequences with the overthrow of the Persian empire by Alexander; with the destruction of Carthage by Rome; with the conquest of Gaul by Clovis; with the taking of Constantinople by the Turks—one might say with the discovery of America by Columbus."

The present anchorage of the three replicas is about one mile upstream from the original site. At present, research shows the proper names for the three ships which brought the settlers to Jamestown to be: *Susan Constant, Godspeed,* and *Discovery.* The misnomer Goodspeed came about in 1890 when the name was miscopied in a contemporary book.

The three ships may be spoken of as square-rigged merchant ships. The *Discovery* is listed as a pinnace or "pinesse," a term used loosely for many types of small ships. The sails are made of linen.

Jamestown Festival Park, where the three replicas of the ships which brought the colonists from England to Virginia are docked, contains a full-scale reconstruction of James Fort, an operating pottery shop, an Indian lodge of 1607, and is staffed with costumed interpreters. It can be reached by taking State Highway 31 south from Williamsburg. It is open daily from 9 a.m. to 5 p.m. and the admission fee for adults is $1; for students, 50 cents; and for children, 25 cents.

THE *Charles W. Morgan,* LAST OF THE WOODEN WHALER

MYSTIC SEAPORT

Mystic, Connecticut
Charles W. Morgan, Joseph Conrad,
L. A. Dunton, Regina M, Nellie,
Emma C. Berry, Annie, Galena,
Estella A, Glory Anna II

A genuine feeling of seafaring ambience pervades the atmosphere of Mystic Seaport, a restoration of a nineteenth-century shipbuilding community. This maritime museum on the Mystic River of Connecticut duplicates a world that our forbears must have known. Ships, the sea, and the fishing industry were vital to the development of coastal communities. Mystic has been the scene of shipbuilding since the 1600's. Some of the earliest settlers were shipwrights who tilled their farms in the summer and in winter built and sailed their sloops and schooners on trading voyages to the West Indies. By 1840, Mystic had become important as a whaling port. Eighteeen whalers left her docks at the height of whaling in 1845 and 1846. During the Civil War, Mystic built 56 transports and other steamships and she continued to build small vessels until 1920.

In 1929, the Marine Historical Association was formed and the Seaport started. It grew from one building and a small collection to over sixty buildings, ships, and formal exhibits on some forty acres of land. In addition to the historic ships moored along the waterfront are the industries and craft shops that supported New England shipping, shipbuilding, and fisheries. Its collection of small craft is the largest in any maritime museum. Examples of early pleasure and work boats, many the last survivors of their types, are displayed throughout the museum either afloat, ashore, or in boat sheds.

The *Charles W. Morgan* is the only wooden whaling ship surviving from the nineteenth-century fleet of American whalers. She was built in

THE WOODEN WHALESHIP *Charles W. Morgan,* LAST OF HER KIND ON PUBLIC VIEW.

1841 at the shipyard of Jethro and Zachariah Hillman in New Bedford, Massachusetts, at a cost of $48,849.85. Originally the vessel was framed and planked with oak and pine. Despite substantial rebuilding from time to time, much of this timber remains in her lower structure. Her present masts and weather deck are of Oregon fir. In overall length she is 113 feet with a 27-foot, 6-inch beam and a depth of 17 feet, 6 inches. Her main truck is 110 feet above the deck. Fully rigged, she is capable of carrying approximately 13,000 square feet of sail. Her gross tonnage is 313.75.

The *Morgan's* whaling ventures took her all over the seven seas. Her maiden voyage began on September 6, 1841. During the voyage, she rounded Cape Horn and cruised the Pacific Ocean. Three years and four months later, with 2400 barrels of oil and 10,000 pounds of whalebone (baleen), she returned to New Bedford, which was her home port for all but 17 years of her active career. Her 37 voyages over the 80-year period ending in 1921 yielded a total of 54,483 barrels of oil and 152,934 pounds of whalebone. Before her "retirement," the *Charles W. Morgan* was home to more than 1000 whalemen. Twenty-one different masters commanded the vessel. Crews averaged 33 for each voyage

THE DORY TRAWLER, *L.A. Dunton.*

THE *Joseph Conrad.*

including officers, seamen, greenhands, etc.

After her whaling days ended, the *Morgan* was preserved by the Whaling Enshrined organization. In November, 1941, she came to Mystic. A popular attraction for visitors are the huge try-pots used for converting blubber into oil. These are forward. Below are the cramped quarters in which her officers and men lived for years at a time.

If any type of commercial sailing craft can be termed truly American in origin, it is the New England sailing-fishing schooner as exemplified by the *L. A. Dunton*. She was designed by Thomas F. McManus and built by Arthur Story at the well-known Essex, Massachusetts, yard and launched March 23, 1921. Sailing to the Grand Banks off Newfoundland or Georges Banks outside of Cape Cod, she soon proved her worth as a fisherman. Tending her dories, she was an able and dependable craft; hove to in a gale, she rode like a duck; coming home, loaded with fish and her lee rail under water, she proved she could carry sail with the best of them. She continued to run to the Banks under canvas until 1935, when she was sold to Canadian interests.

She served her last commercial owners as a carrier of general cargoes. On October 8, 1963, Mystic took official possession and she was restored to her original rig and appearance as a Banks fisherman. A new mainmast, topmasts, gaffs, and booms were produced. The Seaport staff built her a new bowsprit, produced standing and running gear, rigged the vessel, and restored her to her former glory.

The *L.A. Dunton* is now fitted out as a dory trawler, a type which was most common in the American banks fisheries during the heyday of the sailing fisherman. She carries, nested on her deck, ten 14-foot small dories. These seaworthy little boats were lowered over the side when the schooner reached the fishing grounds and rowed off in various directions away from the vessel. Preserved at the Seaport, the *Dunton* is not only an authentic example of the classic development of the American fishing schooner but a testimonial to the humble fishermen and the times in which they lived. Her deck length is 124 feet, the width of her beam is 25 feet, and the depth of her hold is 11 feet, 6 inches. The lower masts are 18 inches in diameter at the deck. The main lower mast is 88 feet, 6 inches long and weighs approximately five tons. The total height of the mainmast, including topmast, is 113 feet above the decks. She is a two topmast schooner and could set eight sails which include jib, forestaysail, foresail, mainsail, fore gaff topsail, main gaff topsail, fisherman staysail, and jib topsail. The frames and hull planking are of oak. Decks are pine and the masts and spars, originally of pine, are fir.

The *Joseph Conrad* is a veteran training ship that sailed under three flags before mooring permanently at Mystic in 1947. Built in Copenhagen in 1882, this 103-foot vessel, one of the smallest full-rigged ships in the world, was designed to accommodate eighty boys in training for the Danish merchant service. In 1905, she was run down in fog by a British freighter and sank, taking 22 young men with her. She was raised, repaired, and resumed her career. Retired after 52 years, she was about to be broken up when Alan Villiers bought her in 1934 and renamed her the *Joseph Conrad*. He took her on a 58,000-mile voyage around the world that lasted two years. In 1937, George Huntington Hartford bought her, added a modern engine, and used her for three years as a private yacht. The U.S. Maritime Commission then secured her as an American training ship until 1945, when a special act of Congress made her a member of the fleet at Mystic.

The *Emma C. Berry* is a 105-year-old, sloop-rigged well smack. She was built in Noank and launched there on June 5, 1866. She is believed to be one of the oldest commercial sailing vessels in American documentation. Built at the R & J Palmer shipyard, she was designed to her owner's specifications along the lines of a Noank

THE SANDBAGGER SLOOP *Annie*.

THE OYSTER SLOOP *Nellie.*

smack, an able craft well known from Maine to the Caribbean. It is sloop-rigged, carrying a large mainsail, two head sails, and, for lighter weather, a gaff topsail. She was an active fisherman until 1924 when she was left on the flats at Beals Island. She was bought for a coastal freighter in 1926. After years of disuse, she was found in Jonesport in 1931 and restored. From 1935 until 1950 she sailed southern waters, and in 1969 was given to Mystic Seaport. She has been restored with the sloop rig for which she was originally built. Her deck length is 47 feet, her beam 14 feet, and draft 6 feet. Her tonnage is 15.76.

One of the most notable craft on display at the Seaport is the Mystic-built sandbagger sloop, *Annie.* Built by D. O. Richmond on the west bank of the Mystic River in 1880, she was given to the Seaport in 1931, the first craft to be acquired. The base of her sail plan measures more than twice the length of the boat, nearly 70 feet from the end of her bowsprit to the tip of her boom. Sandbaggers carried tremendous sail area for their size (*Annie's* is 1313 square feet). They were raced on the Hudson River and along the Connecticut and Long Island shores during the last half of the nineteenth century. *Annie* was champion of them all. Built originally for about $5000, the *Annie* has been twice rebuilt by the Seaport.

The *Galena* is an English-type cutter built in 1913. She is 16 feet on the waterline, yet draws 5 feet, only 1 foot less than her beam. The *Estella A* is a sloop built in 1904 on Long Island. It was used by fishermen and lobstermen for nearly thirty years. She is probably the most authentically restored Friendship sloop to be found

anywhere. The *Glory Anna II* is a cowhorn, a Block Island boat. She is a modern reproduction built in 1948 from lines taken from the first *Glory Anna,* found rotting at New Harbor around 1910. Cowhorns were widely used as day fishermen from 1850 to 1870 and were small enough to be pulled up on the beach at night.

The *Regina M,* although not a true "pinky" schooner, illustrates the most distinctive feature of these craft: the manner in which the bulwarks are carried beyond the stern post and upward to a triangular shaped stern board called the "tombstone." Built in Perry, Maine, in 1900, she was the kind of craft variously termed "Quoddy boat," "Lubec carry-away boat," and by some a "pinky," since natives of eastern Maine are prone to give almost any double-ended craft that designation. At one point in her career the *Regina M* was sloop-rigged. She had been re-rigged as a schooner with a "pink" stern when presented to the Seaport in 1940.

From Long Island comes a different type of craft, the sloop *Nellie.* Used for oyster dredging under sail along the Connecticut shore and in the relatively shallow Great South Bay of Long Island, sloops of this type were characterized by their shoal draft and centerboards. A large and powerful sail plan gave the oyster sloop a turn of speed comparable to that of many yachts.

Mystic Seaport is located on State Highway 27 in Connecticut, a mile from Interstate 95, or Route 1, the Old Post Road. From April through October the hours are from 9 a.m. to 5 p.m. During the winter months the closing is one hour earlier. It is open every day except Christmas and New Year's Day. Adults pay an admission fee of $3.50, children over six years old $1.50.

THE NOANK WELL SMACK *Emma E. Berry.*

THE SCHOONER *Wawona*.

NORTHWEST SEAPORT
Kirkland, Washington
Wawona, Relief, Arthur Foss

In 1897, an almost frantic period of boat building took place in America. In the Pacific, from Puget Sound to California, the boatyards were turning out tall ships to link the countries and harbors of the Pacific into one great seafaring empire.

During that year, the Danish-born shipbuilder, Hans Detliv Bendixson, of Fairhaven, California, launched the three-masted schooner, *Wawona*. It was designed for the lumber trade, and is reputed to be the largest three-masted schooner ever built on the West Coast. Her design made it possible for a small crew to sail her efficiently. Her design was similar to other West Coast lumber schooners of the 1890's, but to the discerning eye she retains the Bendixson look of slightly spoon-shaped bowline, gradual deadrise (rise of the bottom above the horizontal), and just a hint of tumble home (inward inclination above the waterline). Her beam, draft, and sail area are such that she sails without benefit of ballast, a necessity for the quick return passage needed by the lumber trade. She is planked with a species of Douglas Fir known as "Humboldt Pine." She was well dried by the prevailing northwest wind which howled over the Fairbank Peninsula. Her long life can be partially attributed to the fine dried timber used in her original construction. *Wawona* measures 165 feet overall, not including her bowsprit. She has a breadth of 36 feet and her hold has a depth of 12.8 feet. She is classed as a single-decked vessel with a measured gross tonnage of 468.

Relief is a lightship that was launched in 1904 for the Lighthouse Service. She was built in Camden, New Jersey, the first of five in her class. She was launched as Number 83 and christened *San Francisco*. She rounded Cape

THE LIGHTSHIP *Relief.*

Horn and steamed to the city whose name she bore to begin 56 years of continuous service on the West Coast. She eventually became the *Relief* lightship in the U.S. Coast Guard and served at the mouth of the Columbia River. As the more economical Texas Towers, which are embedded in the bottom, became more and more prevalent, the old lightships are fast disappearing, replaced by these steel towers made possible by modern building technology. Over the years, modifications kept the *Relief* up-to-date. Her massive steam engine, originally coal-fired, was converted to oil. She was electrified in 1920, and in 1935 dyaphone whistles were installed on her foremast. Her length is 112 feet, 9 inches, and her beam is 28 feet, 6 inches. Her draft is 12 feet, 6 inches. Her foremast is 52 feet, 9 inches, and her mainmast is 53 feet, 2 inches. She is the only remaining steam lightship in America today. She was decommissioned in 1960 and later acquired for restoration. Her steam engine is in running order.

The tugboat *Arthur Foss* was launched in Portland, Oregon, in 1889, as the steamboat *Wallowa* for the Oregon Railway and Navigation Co. For almost a decade she served the Columbia River, towing sailing ships across the bar and

THE TUG *Arthur Foss.*

into port. In 1898, the *Wallowa* joined the armada of ships, tugs, and barges that headed north following the discovery of gold in Alaska. Among her Gold Rush feats was towing the White Star ship, *Yosemite,* from Puget Sound to St. Michael near Nome. On her return in November, 1898, while towing the bark *Columbia* from Skagway to Seattle, the *Wallowa* was driven ashore in a winter gale, but both the tug and her tow survived. In the years following she logged thousands of miles in Alaska and Puget Sound waters, assisting sailing ships in early day lumber and wheat trade. Following a fire in 1927, her deckhouse was replaced, and in 1934 her steam engine was replaced by diesel. In 1930, she was renamed the *Arthur Foss.* She had the limelight in 1934 when she was used in an MGM picture, *Tugboat Annie,* under the name of *Narcissus.* In December, 1941, after delivering a military tow to Wake Island, she narrowly escaped capture by the Japanese. She was the last vessel to leave the island, returning to Hono-

lulu with no lights and under radio silence. Following military duty during the remainder of World War II, she rejoined the Foss fleet. In 1970, she was donated to Northwest Seaport for historic preservation. The tugboat *Arthur Foss* has a length of 100 feet and a beam of 29 feet. Her gross tonnage was 225.

The Northwest Seaport can be reached by heading north on Interstate 5 out of Seattle. Take the Kirkland Exit off I-5. Cross the Evergreen Point Floating Bridge to Lake Washington Boulevard, following it into central Kirkland. The ships are moored at the central Kirkland waterfront. The Seaport hours are as follows: from September through May, noon to 5 p.m. Tuesday through Saturday. From June through August, noon to 5 p.m. Tuesday through Thursday; Friday through Sunday, noon to 9 p.m. The Seaport is closed Mondays. The adult admission fee is 50 cents, children, 25 cents, and an entire family, $1. There is no charge for children under six.

SAN FRANCISCO MARITIME MUSEUM
Polk Street, San Francisco, California
Balclutha, Eppleton Hall

The story of the San Francisco Maritime Museum is the story of one man's amazing efforts and campaigns to waken San Francisco to its sailing-ship tradition. That man is the Museum's Director, Karl Kortum. Kortum, a seaman and sailer of square-riggers, envisioned a maritime museum that would preserve for all time some of the remaining square-riggers that were still intact but in danger of almost immediate extinction. He fought for a section of San Francisco's North Beach west of Fisherman's Wharf as the location of the Museum. At a time when historic American waterfronts were being de-

stroyed or pinched off by superhighways, Kortum and his band of volunteers actually managed to do something scenically exciting and culturally valid with part of San Francisco's port area.

Kortum and the Museum trustees were given the Aquatic Park Casino, a three-story futuristic bathhouse, a multimillion dollar boondoggle from WPA days. The famous Clark/Spreckels Collection of Ship Models was donated to the Museum and many volunteers scoured the coastline collecting weathered and rusting ship parts and mounting them in the Museum, giving a breath of life to the tiny details of the ship

THE *Balclutha*.

models. They were inspired by the Stockholm's Sea History Museum, where rough-hewn portions of real ships raised from the bottom of the Baltic are on view among the ship models.

The real start of the Museum was the acquisition of the square-rigger *Balclutha*. The Museum Board, or part of it, was strongly in favor of sticking with the conventional museum approach —ship models in glass cases and other interior exhibits—and not getting involved with real ships. Seated in his office on the Museum's third floor, Kortum could look out across the bay and see *Balclutha*, beached and decaying on the Sausalito mud flats. He believed that the acquisition of a real ship, such as the *Balclutha*, was what the Museum was all about, and, moreover, the Museum could be almost self-supporting from the admission fees that the old square-rigger would attract. The *Balclutha* had once sailed in the famous Alaska salmon-packing "Star" fleet. In 1933, she had been bought from the Alaska Packers Association for $5000 by Tex Kissinger, a carnival performer and promoter who had been persuaded by an old sea captain that the best property a showman could invest in would be one of the square-rigged ships of the dwindling fleet tied up in Oakland Creek at Alameda. He renamed her the *Pacific Queen* and painted her like a circus wagon with a silver hull, brilliant red masts and spars, and a gilt figurehead. She was towed forth to begin her new career as an "ark of nautical monstrosities." The *San Francisco News* wrote, "the staid, sedate survivors of the famous old fleet raise their gaunt spars in horror at the antics of their elderly sister."

Kissinger had her towed up and down the coast for nearly twenty years. Early in 1952 he ran her aground in Sausalito, and he died a few months later. The Museum purchased her from his widow, and the Sailor's Union of the Pacific donated over $100,000 in goods and services to restore her. During her first ten years on display, *Balclutha* made $1,000,000 for the Museum, and

STEAM PADDLE TUG *Eppleton Hall.*

there was no longer any need for the Museum to ask for funds from individuals.

The steel-hulled *Balclutha* is a typical British merchant ship of the late Victorian period. In the year 1897, for instance, there were 515 of these steel sailing ships under British registry. Most were familiar to San Franciscans because of the California grain trade. *Balclutha* loaded grain at San Francisco in 1887–89, and 1896, and 1897. She is 256.5 feet in length, 38.6 feet in breadth, 22.7 feet in depth, and 1689 gross tons. The ship, on occasion, carried as much as 2660 tons of cargo and was capable of making about 300 miles a day before a strong fair wind when so laden. *Balclutha* set 25 sails with an average crew of 26 men. The height of the mainmast was 145 feet from deck level to masthead; the length of the mainyard was 86 feet; the length of the ship overall, from end of bowsprit to outboard end of her spanker boom, was 301 feet. The total weight of the gear above deck (the three masts with all yards, sails, and riggings in place) was approximately 110 tons. The

name *Bal* (town) and *clutha* (Clyde River) is the ancient Gaelic word for the site of Dumbarton, the town where the ship's original owner, Robert McMillan, had his home.

In 1970, Scott Newhall, editor of the *San Francisco Chronicle*, added a unique note to the Marine Museum with the presentation of the paddle tug *Eppleton Hall*. Of the same type as the sidewheelers that linked Panama with San Francisco during the Gold Rush, she boasts the same all-but-extinct propulsion—a pair of side-lever engines. Newhall had discovered the *Eppleton Hall* gutted and half-sunk in the mud at a shipbreakers yard in Newcastle-upon-Tyne, England. He bought her and put Bill Bartz and Harry Dring (now restoration director for the Museum) in charge of outfitting her for the 10,000-mile journey to San Francisco. The coal bunkers were ripped out and oil tanks installed for the engines, and she was skippered in and out of twenty ports to find enough fuel for the voracious old steam engines. She sailed under the Golden Gate in March of 1970.

Perhaps the best quote to use in ending this account of the little fleet of the San Francisco Maritime Museum is from Lloyd's of London: "The San Francisco Maritime Museum Association has set an example to the world by bringing history to life through finding means to restore these splendid ships and then allowing them to remain afloat in their natural element."

The San Francisco Maritime Museum is located at the foot of Polk Street in San Francisco. The museum is open daily from 10 a.m. to 5 p.m. There is no admission charge. The ships may be visited daily from 9 a.m. to 11:30 p.m. Adults pay $1.25; children 65 cents.

SAN FRANCISCO MARITIME STATE HISTORIC PARK
Hyde Street, San Francisco, California
Alma, Eureka, C. A. Thayer, Wapama

On Fisherman's Wharf, at the end of the Hyde Street Cable Car Line, is the State of California's unique maritime park where four historic craft are moored and available for public inspection. A "By-Word" electronic system enables visitors to hear narration as they view the vessels.

THE STEAM SCHOONER *Wapama*.

SAN FRANCISCO BAY SCOW SCHOONER *Alma.*

The three-masted schooner *C. A. Thayer* is typical of the lumber carriers developed on the Pacific Coast during the last great days of sail. Big for a three-masted schooner—measuring 156 feet in length, 36 feet in breadth, and 453 tons, with a cargo capacity of 575,000 board feet—the *C. A. Thayer* stands halfway between the little two-masters that scuttled into Mendocino "dog holes" in the 60's and 70's and the last huge four- and five-masters that slid down the ways to meet the shipping crisis of the First World War.

The *Thayer* was built in 1895 by Hans D. Bendixsen at Fairhaven, California. She was one of 35 three-masters built by Bendixsen, and one of 122 built on the West Coast. She was built for the E. K. Wood Lumber Company and named for one of its partners. She operated between their mill at Grays Harbor, Washington, and California, making occasional offshore trips to Guaymas and Honolulu.

She suffered near fatal mishaps when she was driven ashore at Grays Harbor entrance in 1903 and again when her aging seams opened up off Eureka early in 1912. She was towed waterlogged into San Francisco Bay and laid up in Oakland Estuary. She was bought and outfitted by Peter Nelson for the first of her 13 annual voyages to the salmon salteries he operated in Western Alaska. During the War, when bottoms were scarce, she made winter voyages to Australia with lumber cargoes and she summered in the upper reaches of Bristol Bay, Alaska, in company with the great square-rigger fleet of the Alaska Packers Association and other major cannery operators.

Both salmon and sail were on the way out in 1925 when the *Thayer* went to that last haven of West Coast schooners—the Bering Sea codfishery. She was outfitted with dories and a large forecastle for fishermen and for seven seasons went north. After an extended layup in Lake Union throughout most of the Great Depression and brief service as an Army barge during World War II, she went again to the Bering Sea for five post-war voyages. In the fall of 1950 she closed out the eighty-year history of the American codfishery in the Pacific and the age of commercial sail on the Pacific Coast. The Beaches and Parks Division of the California Department of Natural Resources designated the *Thayer* as an historic monument and thus she was made part of the Museum's flotilla.

The steam schooner *Wapama* was built in 1915 at St. Helens, Oregon, by the St. Helens Ship Building Company. Like nearly all of the steam schooners she was at least in part a San Francisco product, for although her wooden hull was built in the forests of the northwest, her machinery was manufactured and installed in San Francisco. The *Wapama* was a fine example of the typical "single-ended" steam schooner (engine room and superstructure aft, in the tradition of the early steam schooners) and she was about as big as a single-ender could be built—205 feet long, 951 tons, with a lumber capacity of 1,050,000 board feet and accomodations for over thirty passengers. For their benefit, she was outfitted with a curving staircase leading down from a spacious lounge into a comfortable dining saloon, a touch well calculated to offset the cramped conditions of her tiny cabins.

A total of some 225 wooden steam schooners were built on the Pacific Coast, the first of the type appearing at San Francisco before 1884. The last was the "double-ended" *Esther Johnson,* built in Portland in 1923. The steam schooners were manned largely by first generation North Europeans, and the fleet came to be known as California's "Scandinavian Navy." The *Wapama,* after she was sold by her first owner, served the White Flyer Line between San Pedro and San Francisco before World War II. She ended her active career under the flag of the Alaska Transportation Company in 1947. As the last surviving wooden steam schooner, she was designated by the Beaches and Parks Division as an historic monument and given to the Museum.

One of San Francisco Bay's unique contributions to the history of American marine architecture was the scow schooner—a type developed around San Francisco in the 1850's to meet the peculiar needs of local navigation. Throughout the last quarter of the nineteenth century the "hay scow," with its towering deck load and its helmsman perched precariously on a ladder, was a familiar sight in the Bay scene. The Museum's *Alma* is a San Francisco Bay scow schooner.

In the horse-drawn era, hay was as essential to the life of a city as gasoline is now, but the scows transported other major cargo as well to communities as distant as Stockton and Sacramento. The flat bottom of the scows gave them a very light draft for a carrying capacity that was generally twice their tonnage, and their tremendously heavy construction permitted them to lie easily on the bottom during loading and unloading operations on tidal flats or creek banks. Scow men were a breed apart and were looked down upon by the deep water fraternity (from which most of them came). They may also have been

THE *C.A. Thayer.*

WALKING-BEAM FERRY *Eureka.*

envied for the comparative comfort of their lives and their profit-sharing pay scale. Their two- or three-man crews were their own longshoremen, and scow schoonermen, not draft horses, plodded up the paths alongside some of the narrow creeks, towing their heavily laden vessels behind, Volga boatman style. *Alma,* the last survivor of this fleet, is 59 feet long and 22.6 feet in breadth, weighing 41.76 tons. Her flat bottom is planked athwartships rather than fore and aft. She was retired in 1957.

The walking-beam ferry *Eureka* exhibits one of the most colorful propulsion machines constructed in the nineteenth century—the vertical beam marine steam engine. The massive simplicity of this three-story engine, transferring the unseen power of expanding steam into monstrous measured movement, brings the spectator and passenger an awareness of the forces propelling him that only sail can rival. The "walking-beam" engine appeared in California waters with the steamship *Senator*—the famous gold boat of the Sacramento. The *Eureka* was the last of San Francisco's vertical-beam ferries, and when she made her final run, in February, 1957, she was the last walking-beam sidewheeler operating in North America.

The *Eureka* was built in 1890 at Tiburon, California, as the *Ukiah,* and operated as a railway car float and passenger ferry for the San Francisco & North Pacific R.R. and later the Northwestern Pacific between San Francisco and Tiburon. In her early years she was held to be the fastest double-ended ferry boat in the world, capable of 18 knots. In 1920, she was almost completely rebuilt as the passenger ferry *Eureka,* a vessel capable of handling 2300 passengers and 120 automobiles. She was lengthened to almost 300 feet; her gross tonnage was 2420, and her extreme beam 78½ feet. With her old 12-foot-stroke engine driving her new 27-foot paddle wheels, she returned to the run from the foot of Hyde Street to Sausalito. She carried her last boatload of commuters in 1941. Another extensive rebuilding in 1953 put her wooden, copper-sheathed hull back in first class shape, but when her massive crank-pin snapped in 1957, the old lady was laid up. She is now part of the Museum's little flotilla.

The Maritime Park can be reached by taking the Hyde Street Cable Car to the Hyde Street Pier, 2905 Hyde Street at Fisherman's Wharf. It is open daily, the year round, from 10:00 a.m. to 6:00 p.m. Adults pay 75¢ and youths 17 and under pay 25¢.

THE SOUTH STREET SEAPORT.

SOUTH STREET SEAPORT MUSEUM
16 Fulton Street, New York, New York

Wavertree, Pioneer, Lettie G. Howard, Ambrose Channel, Mathilda,
Major General William H. Hart, Peking, Alexander Hamilton

In the 1800's South Street was a bustling place of packet ships, sound steamers, fishing schooners, and clippers. Its East River anchorage, sheltered from winds and ice, made it a preferred harbor throughout the era of sail and wooden ships. Far more people came to New York by sea than were born there. As headquarters for worldwide corporations and as a marketplace for money and ideas, and even as a cultural capital, New York is a city that was made possible by the sea.

For a brief period, American ships may have moved more ocean tonnage than the entire British merchant marine. They were newer, bigger, faster, and got full holds every trip. Most of those ships were run from South Street. But one

THE *Wavertree* IN SAN FRANCISCO BAY IN THE 1880s.

hundred years after the clippers, South Street, the street of ships, was dead and became one long parking lot.

In 1966, various preservation organizations decided to restore South Street as a maritime museum. The lovely old brick buildings with their long, sloping roofs and the atmosphere of clipper days were secured and restored. Today, eight ships are berthed at Pier 16, the foot of Fulton Street, as part of the Museum complex.

The prime exhibit at South Street is the square-rigger *Wavertree,* who began her long life at Southampton, England, in 1885. She was a traditional, conservative ship: iron hull, masts, and spars. Her length was 279 feet, and Captain Alan Villiers said she was too big for her three-masted ship rig; she should have been four-masted, carrying double top-gallant sails instead of the big, man-killing single ones. From the beginning she was a wanderer, sail's answer to the tramp steamer, accepting her cargoes where they might be found and working primitive ports which the steamers could not afford to visit. Her last and unsuccessful bout with Cape Horn in 1910 left her with a broken mainmast and yards of smashed rigging and gear. She never carried cargo under sail again.

Gutted, stripped, but still earning her living at the age of eighty as a sand barge in a Buenos Aires backwater, the *Wavertree* was acquired by the Seaport and restoration was begun in 1968 in the Arsenal Naval at Buenos Aires. Six battered plates were replaced and bad plate edges were renewed. Her hull was incredibly sound and scraping of the rust produced clean, gray iron. New bulwarks and beams for the forecastle deck were built and the ship was sandblasted and painted, even to her dummy gunports. She returned to New York, in 1970, to take her place at South Street.

The *Wavertree* is the center and symbol of South Street Seaport, but she is surrounded by a fleet of five other historic vessels, both sail and engine-driven, to make up the largest tonnage

THE *Wavertree* WITH HER RIG RESTORED.

THE *Pioneer*.

of varied ships afloat at any maritime museum.

The active sailer in the Museum fleet is the iron two-masted, gaff-rigged schooner *Pioneer*. She was built as a sloop on the Delaware in 1885 and rebuilt thoroughly in 1966–68 for the late Russell Grinnell, whose family gave her to South Street. She is 58.5 feet in length, 21 feet in breadth, and has a gross tonnage of 43.23. The height of her mast is 77 feet. She carries 2707 square feet of sail. Her function at the Museum is to cruise along the coast as an active training program for young people. She is not open to the public.

The fishing schooner *Caviare* and the original Ambrose lightship lie together. *Caviare's* name was changed to the *Lettie G. Howard* when research into the vessel's background was undertaken. She is the last of the clipper-bowed fishermen who came into the Fulton Slip a few generations ago, and no ship afloat can touch her record of 75 year's service in the North Atlantic fisheries. Her deep hull, subtly curved from a faintly hollowed bow, is of wood and is a good model of what is known the world over as the "Gloucesterman," basically the same hull John Alden gave the schooners that dominated ocean racing thirty years later. She is 84 feet overall, 74.3 feet at the waterline. Her beam is 20.8 feet and her draft 8.9 feet. She was built by Arthur D. Storey at Essex, Massachusetts, in 1893 and was acquired by South Street in 1968.

Her mooring mate is the *Ambrose* lightship built in 1907 at Camden, New Jersey, as "U.S. Lightvessel No. 87, Ambrose Channel." The vessel remained on the Ambrose Channel station until 1932 and saw most of the world's great ships come and go, in peace and in war. She was replaced by another vessel and reassigned to relief service from Base St. George, Staten Island. In 1939, all lighthouse service operations became part of the Coast Guard. After a few more assignments, she became a Coast Guard exhibit at the New York World's Fair, and in 1968 the Coast Guard presented her to South Street as a museum piece.

THE *Pioneer* UNDER SAIL.

THE *Lettie G. Howard*

The steam tug *Mathilda* was built in Canada in 1899, and represents powered harbor craft in the Seaport collection. She was acquired by South Street in 1970. She has a steel hull, is 72 feet in overall length, 20.1 feet in breadth, and draws 11 feet. Her machinery is a 2-cylinder reciprocating steam engine, oil fired. She originally burned coal and had a single-cylinder engine. The steam ferry *Major General William H. Hart* is her companion power craft and was built in 1925 in New York City as the *John A. Lynch*. She ran between Clason's Point, the Bronx, and College Point, Queens. In 1940, she had her last run on the Brooklyn–Staten Island service and was renamed from the *Harlem* to the *Major General William H. Hart*. A second passenger deck was added at that time and she was sold to the Army Quartermaster Corps for Governor's Island service. She was transferred to the Coast Guard in 1965, who in turn donated her to the Seaport Museum in 1970. She is now also used as a marine trades school and is not open to the public.

The *Peking,* a square rigger built by Blohm and Voss of Hamburg in 1911, is the latest acquisition of the Seaport. She had been used as a floating boarding school in England for more than 40 years before coming to South Street. Designed to carry general cargo from Europe to South American ports, the *Peking* "was the last monster that sailed as a merchant ship," to quote her last captain. During the years she was moored in England, six of her lighter yards were given to the Thames Nautical Training College for use on their training hulk. She retains her original fore, main, and mizzen lower and topmasts; fore yard and fore lower topsail yard; bowsprit; and jiggermast (with a portion cut off so as not to be taller than the other three masts). The overall length of her hull is 347 feet (at waterline 321 feet). Her breadth is 47 feet and her tonnage is 3100. She is a four-masted bark with a steel hull. She has 32

THE *Ambrose Channel.*

THE FOUR-MASTED BARK *Peking,*
LATEST ACQUISITION OF THE SOUTH STREET SEAPORT.

THE *Mathilda.*

THE *Major General William H. Hart.*

SCHOONER *Lettie G. Howard* (FORMERLY THE *Caviare*) NOW AT THE SOUTH STREET SEAPORT.

THE *Alexander Hamilton*.

sails for a sail area of 44,132 square feet. The *Peking* is one of the very last survivors of steel-hulled sailing ships.

The *Alexander Hamilton* is a sidewheeler first launched in 1923 at Sparrows Point, Maryland. It was the first dayliner built as an oil burner. Its length is 338.6 feet, with a beam of 77 feet over paddle guards, 42 feet molded, and with a draft of 8 feet, 4 inches. It has a gross tonnage of 2367. An inclined triple expansion engine develops 3900 horsepower and has four boilers. It could carry 4050 passengers. Its interior was decorated with paintings by Herbert W. Faulkner depicting scenes from the life of Hamilton. She made her last regular trip to Albany in 1948 and then travelled from New York to Poughkeepsie. From 1958 to 1962 she made only Labor Day excur-

sions to Albany, and from 1963 made sightseeing cruises to Poughkeepsie. Her last season of operation was 1971, and, in April of 1972, she was towed to the Seaport Museum to join the other ships there.

The ships are only a part of the Seaport complex. It will try to save the existing buildings to assure the preservation of the historic neighborhood with its scale and color and will try to revive the commerce of the street with small shops, restaurants, taverns, and craft activities.

The South Street Seaport Museum is located in New York City at 16 Fulton Street. It is open daily and holidays from 12 noon to 6 p.m. There is no admission fee and it is closed on Christmas and Thanksgiving.

MODEL OF THE SOUTH STREET SEAPORT AS IT WILL APPEAR WHEN COMPLETED.

INDEX OF SHIPS